What People are Saying About
Sleep Baby Sleep

"Thank you so very much for writing this incredible book and technique. This is the best book ever. I especially loved the section that deals with older babies. After my husband and I agreed to break the pattern of dependence that we created, we decided a gentle-toned, firm loving approach would work for our baby. Our couple time was gone. So we bought your book and we are enjoying our freedom again. Thank you so muc̶h̶ ... *Sleep Baby Sleep̶*

... daughter, California

"T ... ok
th ... st
u ... I

"I purchased your book a few months ago. As my baby was then 8 months I was dubious as to whether it could be of help. My daughter wouldn't go to sleep without being rocked to sleep, and then cried a great deal. Well I read the book...and I am the most thankful for all the help...My daughter now goes to sleep on her own, no (pacifier) anymore! If only I had known of this book when my son was little. Thank you again for saving our sanity!!!"

— *Joanne, with a nine month old daughter,*
Seattle, Washington

"I received your book and I can't thank you enough! I am delighted with it!! I have so many friends that have done so many things wrong i.e.: sleeping with baby...some still have an 18 month old sleeping with them...your advice & help is so appreciated! I LOVE the book and we're on our way!"

— *Ally, Great Britain, mother of a ten-week-old boy*

"My experience with the *Sleep Baby Sleep* technique has been a very positive and rewarding one. I began using the technique a few weeks before my baby turned six months old. By the third week of implementing the *Sleep Baby Sleep* technique, my son was sleeping 8, 9 and 10 hours at night! It was incredible. I can now put him to bed and he does not cry at all, and falls asleep before his crib toy turns off (after 10 minutes). The bedtime routine and new sleeping pattern agrees with him, me and the whole family! I feel human again from getting solid sleeping time, and that makes me a happier and more productive person overall, which makes him happy, too. I would recommend this method to Moms and Dads everywhere!"

— *Kimberly, Pasadena, Maryland*

"I can't thank you enough for your book! It's a miracle! My baby is 6 months old, and was addicted to a pacifier and being rocked to sleep. I started the *Sleep Baby Sleep* technique & it took me 2 days to have him sleeping on his own! No lie!!! Thank you so much! I love your book! ...I am recommending the *Sleep Baby Sleep* book for sure!"

— *Shay, six month old boy, Seattle, Washington*

Sleep Baby Sleep

An incredibly simple plan to get your baby and you sleeping through the night

By: Tammy Hussin

© 2005

This book is dedicated with love to my three little angels--Jake, Max and Sam--the best sleepers of all. A special thank you to my loving husband, who without his never-ending patience, love and support, this book could not have been possible.

Book design: Bookcovers.com

Contents

Foreword

Y ou ask what my credentials are. No, I'm neither a pediatrician, psychologist, nor any kind of sleep expert. I'm just a mom (previously corporate lawyer), with three boys of my own. Yes, *just* a mom, whose three boys were all sleeping through the night by eight weeks of age. For me, that's credentials enough. Nothing more than the tried and true, albeit somewhat unscientific, method of a mom who figured out a great plan to get her kids sleeping through the night.

Some said I got lucky with my first child—just the luck of the draw to have an easy baby who slept so well. But by the time my third son was actually sleeping like a baby at seven weeks old, while nearly all my friends were utterly tormented by chronic sleep deprivation, I became somewhat of a local sleeping expert. I began to explain to my friends, and later to my friends' friends, a systematic approach to helping them teach their babies how to fall asleep alone. In no time, the technique that had worked so well for me also worked for many other parents. Since numerous moms had found my approach to be helpful, I decided to write this book to assist any new parents out there who could use a little extra instruction on getting their babies to sleep through the night.

The Sleep Baby Sleep technique works, and best of all, it's nothing more than a basic, easy to implement plan. Through a simple process of teaching your baby how to fall asleep on his own, you will free yourself of the endless stream of sleeping issues that can frustrate you to no end. And that frustration can last for years to come. Once taught, your little one will be able to sleep through the night—and then *everyone* under your roof will rest easier. Your baby *and you* will be less stressed and well rested, and your entire household will benefit.

Another great aspect about this technique is that, as a general rule, you do not have to force your baby to cry himself to sleep in order to sleep through the night. As you may already know, there are way too many books and methods out there that will instruct you to let your child cry until asleep. Sleep Baby Sleep differs in that it offers you a gentle, loving approach that causes very little stress on your baby and you. (Keep in mind, however, that if you are starting this method with an older child, there will almost certainly be crying until you can have your sleeping life back in order. Having to undo and change already established sleep patterns is almost certain to cause tears, and you have to be ready for that.)

People used to marvel at how I could put one of my boys in a crib wide awake after being nursed, give him a blanket and a kiss goodnight, and then just leave the room without so much as a tear being shed. Even today, when my kids are ages 2, 4 and 6, my friends are amazed at the speed and ease at which they go to sleep. Nobody screams, nobody cries, nobody needs to be rocked or have their back rubbed until they are out cold.

After a full day of these three unbelievably rambunctious boys running around, burning what seems like an infinite supply of insurmountable energy, ours is a quiet and peaceful house at 8 p.m. My husband and I get our own time together at the end of the night. Nobody wakes us at 3 a.m. (barring of course the occasional sick child), and we *all* wake up well rested, instead of tired and cranky. The Sleep Baby Sleep approach will enable you, too, to have restful nights and quality time with your partner despite the fact that you have a new baby in the house.

If you weren't lucky enough to have found this book when your child was quite young, then you already know what a toll bad sleeping habits can take on your household. You are intensely sleep deprived, and the relationships around you are probably suffering due to your exhaustion and frustration. Luckily though, the Sleep Baby Sleep techniques can be applied to an older child and you can have tremendous results in a relatively short period of time. In fact, all of the techniques that I offer in this book can be applied to a child of any age. It might take a little bit more time until your older one is sleeping through the night and you're likely to run into some serious resistance, but you *can* do it and it will be well worth your while!

Keep in mind that the Sleep Baby Sleep approach is intended only for use on a healthy, normal baby. If your child has any kind of unusual health, mental or emotional issues, please consult your pediatrician or other health care professional before you use the Sleep Baby Sleep process. Although the technique can safely be applied with any child, it's always best to first consult a health care professional if yours has any particular health or emotional problems.

You will notice throughout the book that I refer to all children in the male vernacular. This is mostly out of habit since I have only boys, but I also thought the book would flow easier simply using a single gender. So if you have a female baby, please don't be frustrated that I neglect to include your little girl.

Lastly, throughout the book I refer to examples of friends and acquaintances whom I have known through the years. I use their parenting experiences and mistakes to demonstrate difficult sleep issues and unwanted patterns of behavior that can easily develop and fester for years. Although the stories are all true, I have changed their names to protect their privacy and anonymity.

Introduction

B ringing a new baby home from the hospital is a
beautiful experience, but it can also be filled
with a multitude of anxieties and frustrations. One
of the major sources of that anxiety is *sleep*. How
am I ever going to get my child sleeping through
the night? How long will it take? When am I going
to get the rest that I so badly need?

The following chapters will guide you, step by
step, and will train you how to gently teach your
baby to fall asleep on his own so that you don't have
to actually put him to sleep. Once your child can
fall asleep independently with this simple process,
he will sleep through the night as soon as he is
physically able to do so. If you don't teach your
baby how to fall asleep without you, then you are
allowing him to need you every single time that it's
time for sleep. That dependence for you could
literally go on for years if you allow it, and will
exhaust you to your core. I've seen it completely
rob mothers of their rationality and sanity. So,
realize and understand that it is all within your

power and control to have your child sleeping without you, and you *can* make it happen if you want it to happen.

The Sleep Baby Sleep technique allows you to incorporate much of the process during the day when your child is still at a very early age. As you will see in the following pages, you will teach your newborn how to sleep on his own for his daytime naps. Once your baby learns how to fall asleep independently during the day, then he will naturally be able to sleep without you during the night. By doing this, your nights won't be painfully filled with trying anything you can think of to get him back to sleep and you can altogether avoid those middle of the night sessions that drive so many new parents to their wit's end.

The Sleep Baby Sleep process is even good for mothers who have only a short maternity leave and are going back to work shortly after the baby is born. You can begin gently implementing the technique with your infant within the first few days. So, for the limited number of weeks that you are able to stay home, you can begin to teach your infant the foundation for sleeping on his own. Even after two or three weeks, you'll notice a major change in your newborn's sleeping habits. Then, when you do have to (or for some of you: want to) return to work, your co-workers will be amazed that you are not consistently bleary-eyed despite the fact that you have a brand new baby at home.

In short, the Sleep Baby Sleep process works something like this: When your baby is somewhere between seven to fourteen weeks old, he will become capable of sleeping through the night without needing to be fed. Some babies take longer simply because physically they are not ready; while others can go the whole night quite early in their little lives. Whether your child is ready at two or at four months old, the transition to sleeping through the night will be downright simple if you've been implementing the Sleep Baby Sleep technique.

If you have used the method throughout the first couple of months of your newborn's life, then your baby has most assuredly already learned how to fall asleep without your help. So, when your child wakes up in the middle of the night on that one magical night when he is ready for uninterrupted sleep, and doesn't need to be fed or changed, he will simply fall back to sleep by himself. As soon as your baby gets to that point, you won't be dragged out of bed and deprived of your sleep to get him back to sleep. You will have taught that little angel of yours to just fall back asleep without you.

On the other hand, even though he may be

capable of sleeping from bedtime to dawn, but you haven't yet taught him how to fall asleep without your help, then who do you think is going to have to put him back to sleep when he starts screaming at 2 a.m.? Of course, it's you. Night after night, long after that sweet little child of yours *could* have an uninterrupted night's sleep, he will need you to get him back to sleep because he hasn't learned how to do it on his own. (And for those of you with an older tot who does need you night after night—well, you know exactly what I'm talking about. And now is the time to take charge and change the pattern!)

If you do not teach your baby how to fall asleep without you, as the months go by you will grow progressively more exhausted. You'll be needed around the clock and robbed of any private time for yourself. Months of this will make you at best quite irritable. Your child will be no picnic either, as he will be cranky and demanding from being constantly robbed of a good night's sleep. And as your nights of chronic sleep deprivation march on, you'll almost certainly begin to resent the fact that you don't get a minute to yourself.

Adding insult to injury, you are highly unlikely to have the energy or the desire to put much time into any of the other relationships in your life. If you're feeling like you don't have a minute to yourself and enduring months of fatigue, it will become increasingly difficult for you to give any of yourself to the others around you. In turn, you'll begin to notice a decline in the quality of your relationship with your spouse or partner. Your partner will grow to be resentful that you save nothing for him, and your relationship will suffer. And this is all because your baby never learned how to sleep without you! Now you have to ask yourself if you get into this situation: Is this really how I want things to go? Is this really making me a better parent?

The important thing is to remember that you not only need to keep your new baby happy, but you also need to care for your own happiness and the others around you. If you make sure that you find time for yourself and you make sure to have some alone time with your partner, you'll be a much happier person and a more compatible couple. Keeping yourself and your partner content should work together with, rather than compete against, your desire to be a loving and nurturing parent. Your new baby should come into your house as an incredible *addition* to your family, and shouldn't take over and rule your house or every aspect of your life. That's not what it's about.

The love and adoration you feel for your new child is exceptionally intense, probably second to none. You most likely have a natural drive to make sure that you are always an attentive and responsive parent, and are determined to provide your child with a safe and loving environment. In the midst of these intense maternal instincts, it is all too easy to forget anyone else's needs, including your own! After all, you now have a "new" love of your life! But you need to figure out the balance. It's important that you try to keep *everyone* happy. And please don't mistake me for a submissive little housewife—believe me, I am far from that in real life. It's just that too many new moms forget to save energy for themselves and for their spouses. This inability to devote any of your energy to your partner will create distance and resentment much quicker than you can believe. Make a conscious effort to avoid letting that happen; the balance and the love in your life will flourish, and everybody wins.

Getting time to yourself, while your baby is sleeping elsewhere, is a great way to achieve that balance. You can still be the great parent that you want to be, without sacrificing the "other" important people in your life. You can tend to your child's every need and have an incredible, loving relationship with your baby; but when it's time for him to sleep—that's when you separate and make some time for yourself. There's nothing wrong with that. Don't allow yourself to feel guilty that you're making your child sleep alone; you have all the many waking hours to make up for it and to be the best parent that you can possibly be.

So when it's time for your child to sleep, it's time for you to separate yourself from him. Don't allow your baby to grow to expect that you will be present each time he sleeps; otherwise that is what you will have to do every night unless and until *you* change that pattern of behavior. If you allow your little one to think that you will put him to sleep every night by rocking him or rubbing his head for a half-hour, then that is what you'll get stuck doing unless or until *you* put an end to it. It is all within your power. It is all within your control. Create what you want in your house, or be willing to endure the consequences.

As a final note before we start, let me tell you that at times the Sleep Baby Sleep technique is going to seem difficult to implement. This is only because there definitely will be occasions when there actually is an easier way to get your little angel sleeping. Sure, if you nurse your child to sleep, or rock him in a chair until he is completely out cold, it might *seem* easier than what I am going to instruct you to do. But if you're not teaching your baby how to sleep by himself, then you'll forever be stuck walking around, driving around, rocking, nursing, or doing whatever ritual it is that you do every single time he needs to fall asleep.

At times it might not seem like my method is all that easy—but trust me, it is! When you are the only mom in the neighborhood getting some shuteye and you're still having a great time with your spouse, you'll be happy you stuck with it. So, let's begin.

Chapter 1

Getting Started - The Sooner the Better

YOUR GOALS FOR THIS CHAPTER ARE:
1. Get started ASAP;
2. Begin using a bassinet;
3. Apply "sleep separation" techniques;
4. Determine a stimulus that soothes your baby;
   – and –
5. Withdraw soothing stimulus.

When you give birth to your new little baby in a hospital, as most people do, you'll be amazed at how little you actually have to do with him. If you so desire, your nurses are likely to let you sleep all night and will bring your newborn in to you only when he's hungry. I'm still astounded at how easy my boys were at the hospital. It seemed like all any one of them did there was sleep, sleep, sleep—just like a baby!

Once we arrived home though, it was quite a different story. All of the sudden we were left with no one to tell us what to do, or when and how to do it. My first son, after acting like an angel at the hospital for two days, screamed his little head off the entire first night we were home. My husband and I still joke about how we looked at each other in the middle of that first night, wondering how we could return this thing who had completely transformed the second we got him home from the hospital! So, although coming home with your new bundle of joy is an unbelievably blissful and electrifying experience, it is undeniably an intimidating time for everyone involved.

Take Michelle, for example. Michelle had given birth to her son, David, by an unscheduled c-section after thirty-six hours of hard labor. Michelle was sore and tired from the trauma of the surgery and the birth, and wanted mostly to just sleep for her three days in the hospital. Michelle's nurses did almost all of the baby tending, while she basically did nothing but nurse when her baby was hungry. When Michelle and her husband got home with their new son, they realized that they didn't even know how to change David's diaper! What a shock it was for them to take over the nurses' responsibilities. Luckily though, it didn't take long for Michelle and her husband to get into the swing of things with David. Michelle used the Sleep Baby Sleep technique with David from the time he was a newborn, and he slept through the night at nine weeks.

__Surviving the First Few Weeks.__ During the first two or three weeks of your infant's life, you can pretty much expect to be in a chronic state of exhaustion. No matter how easy your newborn is, you are almost guaranteed to be worn-out. The entire birthing process in and of itself is draining. Your body will be spent and your bottom sore. If you're nursing, your nipples will be raw. On top of all that, the anxiety of the unknown, coupled with your raging hormones, can be just a little too much for any woman to bear.

The good news is that regardless of how utterly exhausted (no puns intended) and hormonal you are, you will be so overcome with joy and emotion with your new baby that you'll be able to forge ahead no matter what comes your way. (This is true except for cases of postpartum depression, which is not as frequent as supposed and typically passes in a couple of months. New mothers who do suffer from depression need support, and counseling is effective.)

Keep in mind that your newborn will need you for much of your 24-hour day during the first few weeks. This is a time when your baby needs you the most and wants to be as close to you as possible. It's a time to soothe your new little love whenever he needs or wants. Make sure you tend to every need, and endlessly adore him. You are at the beginning of what is likely to be the most incredible bond and most fulfilling journey of your life—so just make sure you start it out with an enormous amount of love and nurturing.

Even though the birthing process is a traumatic experience for you, just imagine what it must by like for your newborn to come out of that nice warm womb. At first that little baby will want nothing more than to be as close to your body as possible, and will not feel comfortable without that reassurance. Two of our three boys slept on my tummy or in between my husband and me for the first few nights. Your newborn will want and need to feel your closeness and you should provide that security for him as much as you possibly can. Likewise, your need and desire to keep your little one ever so close to you will be powerful, especially during the first few days and nights. If you're anything like me, you won't want to leave your new baby's side even for a second. I could barely even give one of my boys up for a couple minutes for a relative to check out our new arrival!

After a few nights go by, you'll begin to get your bearings and have a bit of a routine going with your infant. Once you come out of your fog, you can then slowly begin to create what I refer to as "sleep separation" from your newborn. This process of sleep separation begins by putting your new baby to sleep in a bassinet or a crib next to your bed, instead of keeping him in bed with you. If, after your baby is a few days old, you don't yet feel ready or comfortable separating from him, then let him sleep with you a while longer until you are emotionally geared up to begin.

The important thing to remember is that the earlier you begin the Sleep Baby Sleep technique, the better. The longer you wait, the more time it will take for you to accomplish the goal of getting your child sleeping through the night. If you want to keep your baby in your bed for months, that is most certainly your prerogative—but just be sure that you are ready, willing and able to deal with the consequences of not getting any sleep and *always* being needed. Beginning early makes it much easier for you to teach your child the patterns of sleep behavior that you want. If you start later, you will first have to break the already established patterns of behavior before you can create the new ones that you desire. And believe me, these unwanted patterns of behavior can develop faster than you can ever believe if you let them. Even a sleep pattern that you allow to develop in just the first month or so of your child's life could take some time to undo. So, just be sure to start as soon as you feel like you are willing and able.

Beginning the Sleep Baby Sleep method at a young age also ensures that you'll put the least amount of stress on your child. Teaching your new baby the sleep behavior pattern that you desire from the very start of your relationship will allow for the least amount of anxiety and resistance. Just the mere act of having to change already established behavior can, and probably will, be stressful on your child and you.

Take for example, my friend Mandy. Mandy allowed her new daughter, Michelle, to sleep in their bed for the first four months. By the end of the fourth month, Mandy was living on very little sleep and had become unbearably exhausted. Every time Michelle began to fuss or stir, Mandy would stick a breast in her mouth, desperate to get her little one back to sleep. She was just too tired to even try anything else. It seemed so easy to Mandy to pacify Michelle by nursing her baby. No matter what her daughter needed, it seemed like she instantly quieted down with a breast and would go back to sleep so easily.

Michelle very quickly learned that all she had to do was make a peep and she could be pacified with Mandy's breast. In fact, Mandy's breast became the only form of pacification that Michelle understood was available to her. So Michelle began to demand that breast around the clock. Tired, hungry, frustrated, or whatever— Michelle wanted and demanded that breast, and Mandy was just too tired to do anything but give it to her. This behavior cycle went on for months until Mandy decided to try the Sleep Baby Sleep approach. It took Mandy only about three weeks to teach Michelle how to sleep on her own and to teach her other forms of pacification. Once she learned how to fall asleep on her own, Michelle began sleeping through the night shortly thereafter.

Taking the easy way out in the beginning seemed like the right thing to do for Mandy, since she could quickly get her daughter quiet or get her to sleep by offering up a breast. But what seemed like the easiest path turned out to make Mandy's road so much more difficult and exhausting. Once Mandy finally taught Michelle to sleep without her, she had the time to herself that she needed and wasn't chronically stressed and exhausted. If Mandy had started when Michelle was a newborn, it would have been much easier—but at least she was finally able to have the rest she needed.

So, what if you've waited to start the Sleep Baby Sleep method? What if your baby is older and still not sleeping on his own and you're chronically exhausted? The truth is that no matter how late you begin this process, you still can get your child sleeping without you. If you are committed to the Sleep Baby Sleep technique and determined to have your baby sleeping through the night, then your determination will pay off.

Beginning the Bassinet Approach. As mentioned earlier, your baby should begin sleeping in a bassinet next to your bed at night as soon as possible. Don't worry if you don't have a bassinet, you could use a crib or anything else that basically serves the same purpose. It doesn't have to be a bassinet, but for purposes of illustration, I will always assume that you are using one.

I like the bassinet approach for several reasons. It provides a tiny bit of the beginnings of sleep separation, yet you can still tend to your newborn's needs without ever having to leave your bed. Allowing your baby to be within arms-reach will be great for you, especially since you're probably going to be exhausted and not particularly in the mood to climb stairs or even walk to the next room in the middle of the night. Also, your little one will sense that you are but an arm's length away from him and that you are there to tend to his every need. Quite possibly the greatest aspect to having the bassinet right next to you is that you can begin to teach your newborn how to sleep on his own even when he is all but a few days old.

If your baby is too big or too old for a bassinet, then use the crib when you begin to implement the methods in this book. Not only would a bassinet create a dangerous safety situation for an older child, but he will be too alert and aware of his surroundings to have him right next to you when it's time to sleep. If your baby is more than a couple months old, I recommend starting the Sleep Baby Sleep process with a crib in a separate room. This is because in all likelihood, it will be too difficult to teach your child how to sleep without your help when he is aware enough to notice you in the same room. (See Chapter 5 for details on using the Sleep Baby Sleep process with older babies.)

I was determined to put my first son in a crib in his own room on our first night home instead, of using a bassinet. I felt that having my newborn next to my bed would be too close and would not supply me with the sleep separation that I felt was necessary. Unfortunately, I found myself sleeping at the foot of my son's crib on his floor for the first couple of weeks while trying to accomplish just what I could have done from the comforts of my own bed had I used a bassinet. My baby needed me there with him most of the night for the first couple weeks to learn how to fall asleep on his own, but sleeping on the floor was definitely not an ideal situation. I easily could have accomplished my goals more comfortably.

The use of a bassinet is not obligatory, so follow your instincts if you disagree with my recommendation. You can still accomplish all of the goals in this book without using a bassinet. I only am offering you a method that I have found to be the easiest and most effective. You are the parent, and each parent-child relationship is as different as a fingerprint. So, if you feel that what I recommend to in *any* part of this book goes against your inclinations, then I urge you to go with your gut feeling. You know much better than I do what is best for your particular child, so don't do anything that doesn't seem right for you.

Swaddling your Baby. Most newborns love to be swaddled in a receiving blanket at least for the first couple of weeks of their little lives. Swaddling helps your infant to feel secure after leaving the tight confines and comforts of the womb. I like the nice and thick receiving blankets, although they are more expensive than the flimsy thin ones. The thin ones don't really stay swaddled for any length of time and can be a little annoying. You can find the thick receiving blankets at department stores, or stores like the GAP or Babies-R-Us if you're in the United States.

The nurses at the hospital will most definitely show you how to swaddle your newborn and you will very quickly become an expert at it. Although some infants don't like it, most will be happier and will sleep better being swaddled. You'll very quickly figure out whether your baby likes to be swaddled, and you should swaddle if you can. Although newborns usually only like to be swaddled for a few weeks, it's worth the investment to get yourself at least a few nice receiving blankets. Anything that helps your new baby to sleep better should be a friend of yours!

Getting Started with Sleep Separation. When you do decide that you are ready to have your little one start sleeping in the bassinet, it's a good idea to get yourself into some kind of a routine when you do your last feeding and changing of the night. If you are exhausted and ready to go bed, then have yourself ready for sleep before you give your child what you would like to be the last set of evening activities. This will probably be sometime around 10 p.m. If your child is still a newborn, I can assure you that you'll be exhausted and ready for sleep by the time you do your last feeding. So, be ready for bed and then hopefully you'll be able to get in at least a few good hours of sleep before he wakes up again in the middle of the night, wanting to be fed.

You should wait to feed your baby until you're ready to try to get some sleep as well. Whenever you are ready, turn the lights down low and have it quiet, and then give your child his final feeding of the evening. If you are going to lie down with your baby, it's important that you resist the urge of falling asleep with him on your chest or next to you in bed. Make the commitment that your child *will* spend most of the night in the bassinet and not in your bed.

This won't be an easy task, since you'll be worn out by the end of the day and you'll want nothing more than to let that sweet little angel of yours fall asleep in bed with you. Also, you will realize that the easiest way for you to get some sleep at this point will be to just let your child stay in your bed. Although admittedly, it is the quickest way to sleep at that particular moment in time, you need to begin teaching your baby how to sleep without you. Yes, you will admittedly be making it harder for yourself for the next few nights, but then you'll quickly reap the benefits. Take the harder road for a little while, and believe me it will pay off. If you wait too long to begin using the bassinet approach, you'll wind up much more tired in the long run.

Cindy is a perfect example of why you should use the bassinet as soon as possible. Cindy had put a bassinet next to her side of the bed before her child was even born! She had the best intentions of putting her new baby in it the first night home from the hospital. But when she brought her new little Fiona home, Cindy was exhausted and couldn't muster up the effort to get her newborn out of their bed. Rather than beginning the bassinet approach after a few nights, Cindy instead continued letting Fiona sleep in bed with them. Each night, she took the easy way out by nursing her baby to sleep and didn't use the bassinet at all. Days turned into weeks, and the kid was still in their bed. Each day Cindy promised herself that she would begin using the bassinet that night, but by nightfall she talked herself out of even making the attempt. Weeks turned into months, and her exhaustion from lack of sleep became agonizing. She was cranky and stressed, and everyone in the house was feeling the pressure.

Finally, Cindy couldn't take it any more and felt that she needed to get her bed back. Fiona by then was too big for the bassinet, so Cindy set up a crib in their room. Within just a couple of weeks of little sleep and sheer determination, she had her baby sleeping in a crib and falling asleep by herself. Although Cindy finally accomplished her goal, it would have been so much quicker and much less painful to have used the bassinet technique from the very beginning.

Your mission in using the bassinet is to try to distance yourself from your newborn when it's time for him to sleep. It's critical to understand that sleep separation is a *process*. Do not expect this to happen overnight. Gradually, over the next few weeks, you will teach your newborn how to sleep without you. Day by day, your baby will increasingly grow accustomed to that fact that when it's time to sleep, you will not be there unless you are needed. So, be persistent and consistent, and you'll see results in probably just a couple of weeks.

With these thoughts in mind, you can begin the process of teaching your child how to sleep without you. Once your baby has a full tummy, a clean diaper, and is relatively peaceful, you should place him into the bassinet. If you put your little one down and he is calm, then just move away from the bassinet. If he's quiet, leave him alone—don't stimulate him, don't talk to him, and don't rub him. Always remember that your goal is to have your child fall asleep without your help, so everything you do should further that end.

If you put your little one in the bassinet when he is wide awake, you should expect and in fact anticipate that he will not fall asleep on his own. In all likelihood, your little one will be content and quiet when you first put him in the bassinet, but then as he grows more tired he will be increasingly fussy. If and when your child gets fussy, don't run to his side and pick him up right away; otherwise he will never learn how to happily sleep in your absence.

A little stirring and fussing at this point is likely, and should in fact be welcomed. Look at it as an "opportunity" to help your child learn how to fall asleep without you. The more of these opportunities that you embrace, the quicker you can teach your baby how to sleep on his own. So, even though you're pooped, don't let yourself get frustrated because your baby is fussy and won't go to sleep. Keep your goal in mind, and methodically work toward it by giving your baby the maximum number of chances to fall asleep without you. Don't allow yourself to get discouraged and remember that it's all a process. You will probably have to go through about two weeks of this before your child will stay peaceful once you put him in the bassinet. So, be patient.

Most, if not all, babies are fussy when they are tired and need to go sleep. When your newborn starts to fuss after you've put him down, try soothing him in some way without taking him out of the bassinet. Learning how to soothe your child without picking him up is a key ingredient to the success of the Sleep Baby Sleep process. Don't turn the lights back on and start cooing to him, and don't bring him back into your bed. Keep it quiet with the lights out and don't say a word while you try to figure out how to soothe your child.

I find that a gentle rocking motion to the bassinet is one of the most effective ways to soothe a fussing baby. This technique is especially great if you're in bed, as you can simply reach over to rock the bassinet without even opening your eyes. You might have to rock for quite a while to get your child quiet—so be prepared. Most babies are very soothed by any sort of motion. If motion fails to soothe your particular child, you could try rubbing his little tummy in a slow, circular motion to calm him down, or sometimes, just gently placing your hand on your baby's chest will be enough to quiet him. Do whatever you can that seems to have a calming effect on your child without taking him out of the bassinet. It might take you several nights, or even a couple of weeks to figure exactly what will soothe your little one, but you'll figure it soon enough if you keep at it.

Most newborns have a voracious appetite for sucking during the first couple weeks. So when your newborn is fussy in the bassinet and rocking the bassinet isn't calming him down, you could try offering the tip of your pinky or a knuckle. Again, you can do this from the comforts of your own bed by simply reaching over to the bassinet and letting him suck on your finger. Just do whatever works for you and your child until he is peaceful again.

As soon as you are able to quiet your little one down, then you are ready for the next part of the plan: Withdraw whatever it is that you are doing to soothe your child as soon as he becomes calm. In other words, take away what it was that you were doing to quiet him down, whether it be rocking, rubbing, sucking or whatever. Don't continue soothing your child once he is settled down, and don't wait until your child is fast asleep to stop the activity. Even if your little one is wide awake, withdraw the soothing stimulus the moment he becomes calm.

The reason for this is once you have your newborn in a quiet state, it's a brand new opportunity for him to learn how to fall asleep on his own. If you soothe your baby until he is fast asleep, then he will have missed out on that chance to learn how to fall asleep without your help.

Although I am "anti-pacifier" as general rule, I do believe that there can be a benefit to using a pacifier on a very limited basis during the first couple of weeks of your little one's life (for details on pacifiers, see chapter 3). If you do decide to use a pacifier, the same rule for withdrawing the stimulus should apply. Do not leave the pacifier in your baby's mouth forever. Just like any other form of comforting for your baby, use the pacifier *only* until he calms down, and then take it out of that little sucker's mouth! This way, you can use the pacifier for a beneficial purpose, rather than allowing your child to become hopelessly addicted to it.

Although it's best to withdraw your soothing activity while your child is awake, you don't need to focus on that right away. If your baby does fall asleep while you're trying to calm him down, it's not a big deal. Don't wake him just so you can try to make him fall asleep without you. There's always next time. Focus first on trying to figure out how to quiet your newborn without taking him out of the bassinet. Taking things one at a time with your new baby will allow for the least amount of stress for both of you. So, don't obsess on trying to keep your child awake in order to withdraw the soother on a timely basis. Again, just keep your goal in mind and remember that it takes time.

Try not to get too frustrated if you're unable to calm your baby down while he's fussing in the bassinet. I can virtually guarantee you that there will be many times during the first couple of months that you struggle to calm your baby down, but no matter what you do, he will still be upset. So if you're trying to soothe your child in the bassinet, but nothing you do is calming him down, and his fussiness has now turned into crying, then pick him up. Your little one may simply need to be held or burped, or it may simply be one of many inexplicable crying sessions.

Just make sure that you don't let yourself or your child to get too upset or frustrated. That's not what this book is about, and that's not what parenting is about. You can teach your baby to sleep through a gentle process and you don't need to make him scream to accomplish your goal. Keep trying to calm your child and be persistent, and he (and you) will eventually get it without having to shed too many tears.

Many times, especially during the first couple weeks, your newborn will fall asleep while you are trying to calm him down. In that event, stop whatever soothing technique you were doing and hopefully he will stay asleep. But if your baby begins to stir again, don't do anything right away. Let him fuss a little bit before you try anything again. You might be pleasantly surprised to find that your little one will fuss and stir for a while, but then go back to sleep on his own.

This concept is really the inner key to the Sleep Baby Sleep process. This is how you lay your foundation for teaching your child how to sleep without you. It won't work the first night, but at least you are beginning to show your newborn how to sleep without you. Night after night from this point on, you should continue this pattern: Withdraw the soothing stimulus when your baby is calm and still awake, and repeat it throughout the night unless you're just too exhausted. Do it as often as you can, and the more you do it, the quicker your child will be able to fall asleep without you. Unfortunately, the reverse holds true as well—the less you apply the technique, the longer it will take to have your baby falling asleep without you. You have to push yourself to do it though; especially in the middle of the night when all you want to do is just get a little sleep. Just don't forget—it's the short-term pain for the long-term gain.

You may be feeling too tired to deal with trying to soothe your newborn on any particular occasion. You will undoubtedly be going through a lot of hormonal changes after your baby arrives and your tolerance level for stress might be a little low. Don't worry—you can always try again next time when you are feeling better equipped to deal with it.

During the first couple nights, it could take you *hours* to calm your child down enough to even get him into the bassinet. Newborns have countless episodes of unexplained crying, and you need to work around these periods while trying to implement the sleep techniques. Once you are through the first couple of nights, it might take you an hour or so of doing this before you can finally get your infant to sleep. This will probably continue for the next couple of weeks. The more persistent you are, the faster your baby will learn to be an independent sleeper. So it's up to you. Take the challenge if you're up for it, or wait until the next time when you're feeling better equipped. The more you use this technique, the faster you will see results; the less you use it, the longer it will take.

As a side-note, you need to make sure that your child isn't fussing because he is hungry or needs you for some other reason. If your baby doesn't have a full tummy and it's been a couple hours since you've fed him, then you might see if hunger is the reason. You might be surprised that even after just an hour or two, your little one may very well be hungry again. But watch out—you need to trust your intuition to figure out whether your baby really is hungry or just wants a little pacification. You'll know that your baby was hungry if he gobbles down your entire milk supply as soon as he latches on. But if your child latches on to your breast and falls asleep within the first minute, then he probably just wanted to be pacified to sleep.

Beware of becoming a human pacifier! If you nurse your little one every time he fusses or if you nurse your baby to sleep too often, then he will get used to that behavior very fast. Your baby will all too quickly grow to expect a breast stuck in his mouth every time he makes a peep. You'll wind up in a situation where you are nursing your child all day and all night even when he's not hungry. So, if he's hungry, by all means feed him—but if he's not, watch out! Make sure you focus on figuring out other forms of pacification, or you'll be nursing around the clock before you know it.

Although everything at this stage is so very new for you, you'll soon be able to figure out your baby's cues. Your maternal instinct will kick in and you'll begin to understand whether your child needs to be pacified or is just plain hungry. Trust your instincts – when it comes to a mother's intuition, you'll almost always be right.

Chapter Review

(Don't leave this chapter until you have mastered the following concepts)

1. Get your baby out of your bed and into a bassinet as soon as possible;
2. Understand the "sleep separation" techniques;
3. Figure out what soothes your baby;

– and –

4. Understand how and why to withdraw the soothing behavior

Chapter 2

Daytime Rituals

YOUR GOALS FOR THIS CHAPTER ARE:
1. Apply the Sleep Separation technique during the day;
2. Put your baby to sleep awake;
3. Teach your baby how to fall asleep alone;
   – and –
4. How to cope with the witching hour fussiness.

In this chapter, you will begin to learn how to use the daytime hours as an additional teaching ground to help your child discover how to sleep independently. Over the next few weeks, these day and night time methods will work together to teach your little one how to fall asleep without you and to sleep through the night. The daytime technique will also help to ensure that your child begins to take long, solid naps during the day, so that you can begin to find some time for mommy.

Many new parents are inclined to put their babies to sleep by nursing (or a bottle) or rocking. This is because initially it actually *is* much easier to get your child to fall asleep this way. Admittedly, it is seemingly effortless to simply rock or nurse your newborn to sleep, and much more difficult and demanding to put him down in the bassinet. And trust me, it will be ever so tempting for you to let that little angel fall fast asleep by rocking him or on your breast (or a bottle), and then to lay him down to nap or hold him in your arms. This is especially enticing since you will be pooped and yearning to have your little one sleeping using the quickest means possible. You must resist this temptation! The methods that initially appear to be the fastest and easiest will ultimately become your nemesis and are bound to create a more exhausting scenario for you both in the long-run.

If you nurse or rock your child every time he needs to sleep (or even most of the time), he will never learn how to do it without you. Not only will your presence be required each and every time you put your child to sleep, but every time he wakes up, he will demand your presence to *get* him back to sleep. When your little one wakes up in the middle of the night (even when he is two years old) it will be *you* putting him back to sleep each time if he has never learned how to do it himself. This is a vicious cycle that needs to be avoided (or, if you're already in it, then it needs to be changed!).

Additionally, the longer the pattern goes on, the more difficult your child will be to get to sleep. It could take you literally hours just to him fall asleep at night. Imagine how stuck you will feel when you have to go into your kid's room every night at 3 a.m. to rub his back for an hour just to get him back to sleep. After a year or two of this, you will both be exhausted and cranky, as neither of you will get the amount of sleep that you need. This is no exaggeration, as some of you already know all too well.

Jackie sought my help when her baby was four months old. They had quickly gotten into some bad sleeping routines and both of them were tired and cranky nearly every day. From the time her daughter was born, Jackie almost always nursed her to sleep. I was not at all surprised when she told me that her little one was not even close to sleeping through the night, and still woke up three or four times a night to nurse. Whenever her little girl woke up, Jackie simply nursed her back to sleep.

For the first few weeks, Jackie didn't mind the nursing-to-sleep routine. She saw it as the only way to get her baby to sleep, and thoroughly enjoyed the bonding of nursing and sleeping with her little bundle of joy. But as the little girl got older and Jackie became increasingly exhausted, the situation became intolerable. Jackie didn't like that she had basically turned herself into a human pacifier and was needed around the clock. She was beginning to feel like she was on a very short leash. It became increasingly difficult for Jackie to have her baby sleep for any stretch of time without needing her breast. Her daughter woke up much more frequently than was necessary and everyone in the house was tired and cranky.

Things really changed once Jackie began to teach her daughter how to fall sleep on her own and without a breast. Her little one naturally began to sleep longer and better, and everyone in Jackie's house was better rested. Her child slept through the night after being on the Sleep Baby Sleep routine for just three weeks! Everybody finally got the rest they needed, and Jackie got some time to herself while her daughter finally learned how to rest peacefully.

Putting your baby to sleep awake. Your primary goal is to learn how to put your baby to sleep while he is still awake. It's much easier to conquer this goal is during the daylight hours than during the night. You will be more alert, more sane (at least theoretically), and have much more patience than when you're burning the midnight oil trying to figure out how to with a child who won't go to sleep.

If you have a newborn, you'll probably want to wait until he is about three weeks old before you begin the daytime sleep methods. The first few weeks with your infant will pretty much be a blur, and you'll be busy enough just trying to keep your head above water. By the time the third week rolls around, your child's naps will be getting a bit more predictable and you'll begin to feel like you're beginning to come out of your fog. If your baby is already older, then you know better than I that *now* is the right time to start!

Once you've determined that you are ready, you need to first figure out a good location for your little one to take his naps. The ideal place for your new baby to sleep is somewhere right in the midst of the activity and daily noise of the house. You want him to learn how to be able to sleep through all kinds of commotion from day one, and napping him in the center of the action is a great way to accomplish that. Your child won't wake up from any little sound that he hears, and will sleep more soundly and wake up better rested. So, find a bright, noisy spot for your little to nap.

Your baby's naps will rarely be interrupted as the months go by if you can get your baby sleeping through anything. I can promise you that you'll soon place a very high value on the time that you get when your little angel is napping, and you'll be as cranky as him if a nap gets cut short. If you keep it too quiet while that sweet thing of yours is napping, then the first time the phone rings or a cabinet closes he'll wake up screaming and be crabby because he didn't have a full nap.

If you can move the bassinet into your main living area, then you could have your baby nap in there. If it's too cumbersome to move the bassinet back and forth, then use some other space around the house. You could even do the daytime naps in a stroller or a car seat. If you don't have other kids or animals, then a blanket on the floor will work just fine. I've even known a parent or two to cushion a laundry hamper with a few blankets to use as a napping space. (If you're starting the Sleep Baby Sleep process with an older, more alert child, then he should not be napping with you in the same room. Instead, refer to Chapter 5 for other techniques on starting with older babies.)

Putting your child down for a nap while he is still awake can be a difficult task, especially if you have a newborn. Your baby should always take a nap or go to sleep at night with a full tummy, as he is likely to sleep better and longer on a full tummy. The tricky part about this is that while you are feeding your little one, he will want nothing more than to close his little eyes and fall asleep in your arms. Your milk (or formula) is oft times like a sedative and it will often pose quite a challenge to keep him awake through feedings. So you'll probably have to accomplish this goal with some ingenuity on your behalf.

I do have a few tricks up my sleeve that may help you to keep your new baby awake until after you feed him: The best trick is to try changing your child's diaper after you feed him, rather than before or in the middle of the feeding. Typically, most parents do the burping and changing half-way through a feeding, then by the time they are done your angel is likely to be out cold. Instead, try changing your little one after you're all done feeding him (although burping at the half-way point is still a good idea). This will oft times stimulate your baby enough for him to be at least semi-conscious when you lay him down to sleep.

If you continue to change your baby at the end of the feedings, you'll become increasingly skilled at keeping him awake over the course of the next couple of weeks. Don't fret if your baby drifts in and out of sleep while he's feeding—that is pretty much to be expected. So long as you try to have your little one even partially conscious when you're done, then you've accomplished your mission and you can try to put him to down for a nap while he's still awake. Tickling works great, too. You can tickle your little one's feet or tummy to try to keep him awake while you're feeding him.

If you have a newborn, keep in mind that there will be many times that you simply will not be able to keep him awake until the end of the feeding. That's okay. It is *not* critical that your little baby is awake every single time that you set him down for a nap; rather, just let it be the general goal that you are working toward. Remember, it's all a process and none of this will happen overnight. It will take you at least two or three weeks of this before you will really see results, so be patient with yourself.

If you are just too tired to try these methods on any given occasion, or if no matter what you do you simply cannot keep the baby awake, then just try again the next time. It is not an absolute necessity that you keep your baby awake every single time in order to have success with this process. Keep trying and you will achieve your goals—I promise you. I caution you, however, that if you take the easy way out too many times, it will take you all the longer to teach that little angel of yours how to sleep without you. Even though you don't have to implement this method at every instance, ensure that it is your basic goal to put your baby down for a nap while he's awake for every possible occasion.

This is a good time to remind you that you do not have to be by your child's side when it is time for him to sleep. You don't need to be with your baby every single second in order to be a wonderful and nurturing parent. Of course, you want to be loving and giving, but at the same time you need your own space and time for yourself. The perfect time for you to get that breathing room is when your child is sleeping.

Naptime is the ideal opportunity for you to rejuvenate and have some private time. Unless you take advantage of this opportunity for yourself, you won't find any at all. Don't allow yourself to be on demand 24 hours a day, 7 days a week; otherwise, you'll tire of it quickly. Let your child get used to you not being there when it's time for him to sleep. Hopefully, you'll be able to be there for your child, all other times, for a lifetime. But when it's time to sleep, say good-bye, walk away, and most of all *don't* feel guilty!

As a side note, keep in mind that babies cry for a multitude of reasons, and many of these tearful episodes are completely inexplicable. When your little one cries, you will at first be baffled as to why. There will be countless times that you simply will never know. No matter what you do to try to calm your child, it won't work. It is these times that you simply need to hold your baby and ride out the storm. Sometimes it will go on for what seems like an eternity, and on other occasions it will pass quickly.

As your new baby develops, the crying will decrease and will also become more intuitive. Crying is your baby's primary means of communication. Instead of allowing yourself to be frustrated, see if you can begin to figure out your baby's signs and cues. Your maternal instincts are stronger than you might believe, so be sure you trust in them. Listen to what your little one tells you even though he can't yet utter a word, and you will naturally become increasingly adept at understanding what he wants and needs. In the meantime, allow yourself the patience to figure things out. This is all so very new for both of you and the inexplicable crying sessions can grate on your nerves if you let it—so be careful.

Usually when your baby cries, he is either hungry or tired. You'll notice as your newborn gets a bit more mature that he will begin to grow tired and fussy at predictable times throughout the day. At first, your baby will take many short, little "cat naps". Then as he gets a little older, the cat naps will begin to condense into three or four longer, deeper naps. Each of these naps, no matter how short or long, is a chance to teach your baby how to fall asleep alone. So, each time, try to keep your little one awake through the feeding so that you can seize every opportunity possible.

Just Walk Away. Once you've gotten your little sleepy one to stay awake (or even semi-conscious), and he's got a full tummy, a clean bottom and is relatively calm, you can now put him down for a nap. Put him down wherever it is that you've chosen for the nap—and then just walk away! That's right, just leave. If you are confident that it's time for your baby to sleep, then put him down and walk away.

Once you do walk away, see if your baby can fall asleep without your help. Similar to the bassinet routine at night, teaching a child how to fall asleep without you for his daytime naps will probably take several weeks to accomplish. At first, your little one is likely to have a period of peacefulness, lying there on the floor or wherever, and then will become increasingly fussy as he grows more tired. Because your newborn does not yet know how to fall asleep without your help, he will fight his sleep and grow progressively agitated as he tires.

Don't give in to frustration if the child doesn't fall asleep at first, but fusses due to tiredness. Instead, try to soothe him while he is still lying down. Just like when your child is in the bassinet at night, soothe him without picking him up. Implement the same type of soothing techniques that were previously discussed, and try your best to figure out something that calms your baby down. Whatever you do, make sure you do not wait until your little one is crying and screaming for you to pick him up. If you conclude at any particular time that there is no way that little angel of yours is going to calm down by trying to soothe him, then pick him up and try again the next time.

If you allow your baby to get so frustrated that he builds into a full blown crying episode, then it will be very challenging for you, if not down right impossible, to calm him down. It is not necessary to force either one of you to get upset and frustrated. You can still accomplish the goals in this book while maintaining a more peaceful and less stressful environment. So, at the point that the fussiness begins to turn into a full blown crying session, after you've done all you can do to soothe him, then pick that little rascal up. You can always try the next time when your baby goes down more peacefully. Don't make the poor thing cry it out! It simply is not necessary with an infant. If your baby has become so upset that he needs you, then pick him up and just try it again the next time. Don't torture yourself or your baby—that's not what parenting is supposed to be and not what this book is all about.

On the other hand, if your child is not crying but is merely extremely fussy, try the calming techniques that we discussed earlier—rubbing his little tummy, a soft hand, a pinky or a knuckle, or yes—even a pacifier if you must. Don't go to your child if he is merely fussing or flailing about. It's a great opportunity for you to get your little angel to sleep without your help, so give it time. Keep at it, don't give up, and continue trying to figure out something that works to calm your child down without picking him up.

Don't forget that it is likely that you will have to make many attempts over the course of the next couple weeks to achieve your mission. So, don't get frustrated. With each attempt, you are giving your baby yet another chance to learn how to fall asleep on his own, so be sure to take advantage of each and every occasion. But be patient! Keep your mission in focus and continue to work toward it. It *will* work for you if you are diligent and consistent.

These nap rituals will continue on a daily basis over the course of the next few weeks until you finally feel like you are gaining some ground. The combined forces of the night time and the daytime routines will have your child falling asleep on his own probably within about two or three weeks. You'll be amazed how quickly you can establish the sleeping patterns that now seem so out of reach.

On the occasions that you are simply unable to calm your baby down and you have to pick him up, you haven't necessarily missed out on an opportunity to teach your child how to sleep without you. If you do have to pick him up, then once he has settled down and you are fairly certain that he still needs to sleep, try putting him down to start the process all over again. Just as before, don't go back to your little one until he gets pretty fussy, and again try to soothe him without picking him up. Remember that it's all a process that won't happen overnight, and be sure to keep your goal in sight without getting too frustrated.

Most babies need a great deal of sleep. It's not uncommon for your newborn to sleep more than he is awake. Keep in mind, however, that there are only a few babies out there who simply need less sleep than the rest of them. If you cannot get your child to nap, you should know that there is only a slight possibility that you have one of these sleepless children. More likely, you simply need to teach your little angel how to sleep better and how to fall asleep without you.

A good way to figure out if you have a newborn who doesn't need a lot of sleep is to see whether he is happy without a lot of sleep or whether he is chronically cranky. If your child is fussy and crying all the time with little sleep (as most are), then he probably just needs more sleep and you need to focus your efforts on teaching him how to sleep better. If the little bundle of joy is basically happy most of the time and it is really only you who is the only exhausted one, then you unfortunately might have a kid who doesn't need much sleep. If that is the case, you should still stick to the Sleep Baby Sleep method, but don't expect to find a lot of time to yourself throughout the day. Even though your child might not need much daytime sleep, almost all babies should be able to sleep through the night and you can focus your efforts on ensuring a restful night-time sleep.

Betsy's son just didn't need a lot of sleep, and it took her quite some time to figure this out. She tried for months to get her son down for a nap, but no matter what, he wouldn't sleep. Regardless of what she did and how much she applied the Sleep Baby Sleep approach, he wouldn't nap. When Betsy sought my advice, I pointed out to her that her little boy didn't seem tired. Even though Betsy was ready for her baby to take a nap, unfortunately he had a different agenda. With my advice, Betsy was able to eventually have her son to play quietly in his crib for an hour each day, but it most certainly was a frustrating situation for her.

As mentioned earlier, this predicament is not a common one, as most children need a generous amount sleep as a prerequisite to being happy. Only a few babies don't need much sleep, so don't make the excuse that yours simply will not sleep. The more likely scenario is that your child has never learned how to sleep when he is tired. A baby like this will constantly fight his sleep, and will wind up in a chronic state of crankiness. This causes havoc for the entire household. So, figure out what kind of kid you have and what it's going to take for you to institute some changes.

Don't be a "Debbie" *Debbie's son, Matthew, was two years old and was a chronically cranky kid. Matthew rarely took a nap (although he almost always needed to), and by the age of two he still woke up several times* during the night. Debbie had gotten herself into the terrible habit of having to lie by Matthew's side at night until he was deeply asleep. For well over an hour each and every night, she crawled into bed with Matthew and rubbed his back until he was completely out cold. It was only when Matthew was in a deep sleep that she could even attempt her escape from his room. On most nights though, Matthew would sense Debbie's absence as soon as she left the room, and would wake up screaming until Debbie compliantly returned to his bed. Because of this, Debbie wound up sleeping in Matthew's bed for the entire night almost every night.

Debbie's pattern of sleep behavior with Matthew started as soon as Matthew was born and things just snowballed from there. Instead of taking the time to teach Matthew how to sleep independently from the very beginning, Debbie took the easier way out. It seemed so easy for Debbie when Matthew was a few weeks old to just nurse him to sleep and to keep him in bed with her all night. As a result, she wound up having to always nurse Matthew to sleep. When Debbie tried to put Matthew is his own crib, he would scream and cry until she gave in and brought him back into her bed. Not only would Debbie nurse Matthew to sleep, but she continued nursing him throughout the night whenever he made as much as a peep. Matthew never learned how to sleep without Debbie (or to be without her at all for that matter), and demanded her presence twenty-four hours a day.

Matthew never learned how to take naps during the day. No matter how tired he was, the only way Debbie could get Matthew to nap was either by driving him around in the car for over an hour until he finally fell asleep, or by nursing him to sleep and staying in bed with him for the entire nap. On the days that Debbie had neither the time nor the inclination to do either of these things, Matthew was insanely tired and agitated the entire day until she could finally get him to sleep by again lying by his side in bed at the end of night.

Aside from taking what seemed like the easy way out, there was also a certain amount of self-imposed guilt that made Debbie feel pressured to be with her son at all times. Debbie felt that she had to be with Matthew twenty-four hours a day and keep him happy in order to be a "good" mom. She felt that she needed to do this for Matthew because she felt too guilty doing it any other way. So, this supreme sacrifice had Debbie catering to her child's every whim (and every whimper) at any hour of the day or night.

What Debbie failed to realize though was that this ultimate sacrifice for her son, coupled with her *chronic sleep deprivation created a hostile environment that loomed over their house. Debbie was angry, frustrated and overly-tired. The ironic part of this whole thing is that Debbie would have been a "better" mom (and partner) if she had just gotten some sleep and a little bit of time to herself. Debbie had absolutely no privacy, and felt pulled in every direction. Her patience with her husband and her child was very short, and Debbie was frazzled.*

As time marched on, Debbie began to resent how demanding and difficult Matthew had become. The truth of the matter was though that Matthew was not actually a "difficult" baby; rather, he was simply conditioned to expect to get anything he wanted from Debbie, and she enabled him to get it. Debbie constantly gave in to her son's demands, and so Matthew learned that he could have anything from his mother at any time of the day or night if he just hollered loud enough. Mommy's behavior actually rewarded Matthew for screaming, and he was well on his way to becoming a tantrum-throwing child.

Even when Debbie was at her wit's end, she was just too tired to do even try to institute any changes to what had quickly become a very tough go at motherhood. Debbie had been up so many times every night for two long, hard years, and had become utterly exhausted and bitter. To make matters worse, she was almost always robbed of any quiet time with her husband. You can just imagine the crankiness and stress that was in Debbie's house.

So now ask yourself: Was Debbie a "better" parent because she didn't make her little one sleep alone? In my opinion, everybody in Debbie's house, including the child, would have been much better off had she done things differently. The saddest part about Debbie's situation is that she had the power to avoid the entire situation. Debbie *allowed* every bit of it to happen. It's not that she was a bad person or a bad mother—it's just that from the time Matthew was born, Debbie never took the time or the initiative to teach her son how to sleep without her. Two whole years of tension in their house could have been completely avoided if only Debbie had taken just a simple few weeks to make Matthew sleep on his own. It was all within Debbie's control to institute changes at any time along the way; instead, she let bad habits develop for way too long and then never had the energy to reverse them.

If you want your house to be more peaceful and less stressful than Debbie's, then make sure you don't let this happen to you (that is, if it hasn't already). It's easier than you can ever imagine allowing yourself to fall into bad patterns of behavior with your child. Even if you're not a complete "Debbie", make sure you don't allow yourself to become any part of her either. It's just too easy to nurse or rock your little angel to sleep every time instead of teaching him to fall asleep on his own. It's just too easy to let yourself be lazy and allow unwanted behavior patterns to develop. Once these patterns develop, they are ever so difficult to reverse.

There are more Debbies out there than you can ever believe. I'm sure you probably know a few. And if you already have become one—then *now* is the time to change your trend. It's never too late to make reparations and get rid of unwanted behaviors. And remember not to allow yourself to think that you're a "bad" parent for making your child sleep independently. It's okay for you to have some space from your child, and in fact your entire house will benefit from it.

So, make sure you take the time *now* to separate yourself from your child when it's time to sleep, regardless of what has already transpired. It's the Debbies out there who picked their babies up every time they made a little peep, and never taught them how to sleep on their own. Make sure that angel of yours doesn't stay in bed with you for too long—it's the Debbies out there who were just too tired to put their babies in a bassinet and allowed their babies to sleep next to them. Make sure you don't nurse your baby every time he stirs or fusses, as it's the Debbies out there who wind up with a baby who nurses on demand twenty-four hours a day.

Although beyond the scope of this book, I think it's an appropriate time to add my two cents about child rearing in general. You need to make sure that you don't allow this little angel of yours to turn into a devil. Don't let your child think that he can get every little thing that he wants (including demanding your presence around the clock), or he will become increasingly difficult to handle. Instead, enable your child to develop self-discipline and to have respect for your boundaries, even at a very young age.

It starts very early, and has very long lasting effects. The way you allow your child to act now will affect how he behaves for a lifetime. Teach your child discipline and rules from the start and you won't wind up with a toddler who throws tantrums, or an unruly and disrespectful seven year old, or a trouble-making teenager. In other words, don't let your kid become a brat. It only gets worse as your child ages and you are more in control than you think. So, make some decisions early on as to the type of child you want to have in your house, and then work to create it.

The bad sleeping habits that you allow to develop with your little one are difficult to live with, but even tougher to reverse. Teach your baby how to sleep on his own *from the start* and I promise you, you won't be a Debbie! Just take the few weeks now—no matter how old your child is—and the coming years will be so much easier. Parenting in and of itself is enormously challenging—don't make it even harder than it already is by suffering from chronic sleep deprivation for the next couple of years. Get some sleep and some time for yourself (and your partner), and you'll find that you will be a much better parent than if you make the supreme sacrifice of catering to your little one twenty-four hours a day.

The Difference between Night and Day. It is important to make sure your baby figures out the difference between day and night soon after birth. Almost all newborns have their days and nights mixed up for the first couple weeks of their little lives. If you take the right steps, you can help your child to quickly work through this confusion.

As mentioned earlier, you should nap your infant in the center of the action in your house. This will also help your newborn to quickly understand the difference between night and day. It's also a good idea is to keep music on throughout the day. If you have other kids, don't make them tiptoe around. Go about your daily routine with your sleeping baby in the center of all of the action. Do the dishes, run the vacuum, or whatever. Don't put your child in a separate room and don't try to make it dark and quiet during the day. So make lots of noise and keep it nice and bright, and your little one will sleep better and will be able to quickly figure out the difference between day and night.

Exactly the opposite holds true for the nighttime. You should always try to have it as dark, and as activity-free and quiet as possible when you are ready for your child to go down for the night. Keep your other kids away (if you have any) for the last feeding. Close yourself into a dark room if need be to keep it calm.

When you feed and change your newborn in the middle of the night (as you will be doing for at least the first couple of months), keep the room as dim and as calm as possible. Don't turn on the light (unless you have to clean a messy poop), don't stimulate your baby, don't talk to him at all; just do what you have to do, put him back in the bassinet or crib, and then leave. Keeping it dark and quiet in your child's room will help him to understand that the night is for sleeping, and will help him to figure out the difference between night and day as quickly as is possible.

<u>Coping with the Witching Hour.</u> No matter how "easy" your new baby is, you are likely to run into several weeks of intense late afternoon fussiness. Many parents loosely refer to this dreaded time as the "witching hour". Unfortunately, this witching hour fussiness tends to fall right around the same time that you are trying to put dinner on the table and when you are most fatigued from the day's events. This period usually entails a couple hours of varying degrees of a newborn "melt-down".

The witching hour crying typically begins when your child is about two to three weeks old, and continues on a daily basis for at least a few weeks and sometimes even longer. It is a difficult thing for new parents to cope with, and can cause a lot of stress if you let it. Some babies scream their little heads off every afternoon for an hour or two no matter what you do for them; others just are fussy and crabby and need to be held the entire time.

The good news is that these episodes typically only last for a few weeks and then dinner-time gets a little easier for everyone involved. The bad news is that while you're going through it, there's oft times *nothing* you can do to make your little one happy. No matter what you do to try to alleviate the fussing, the poor thing will do nothing but fuss and cry for a couple of hours.

It's important to understand that the incurable distress of the witching hour makes it a bad time to try out any sleep separation techniques. Your child in all likelihood will simply be too fussy, and trying to separate yourself from him at this time will cause nothing more than intense exasperation for everyone.

Instead, try anything you can to calm your baby down. You could see if using an automatic swing or rocker soothes your child, as it is very helpful for many babies. Sometimes the swinging motion in and of itself can be sufficient to quiet him down. But a swing doesn't always help during the witching hour, and you might just wind up having to hold your little one for the next few weeks until these periods of inexplicable fussiness subside.

Using a sling or other type of carrier can also be useful for you when you have an inconsolable baby. A carrier at least enables you to free your hands and be productive while giving your little angel the movement and the closeness that he craves while he is so unhappy. It can also help to alleviate the tortures of the witching hour, since you can at least get a few things done around the house instead of just walking around with your child for two hours. Whatever you choose, be prepared for some significant stress on the house for the next couple weeks until it works itself out and fades away.

Sleep Brings more Sleep. It's a common misconception to think that if you keep your child awake from the late afternoon to bedtime that he will go to sleep easier and sleep better at night. *Not true.* In fact, the truth is that sleep begets sleep. The more your young child sleeps, the more he will sleep. Sometimes my boys would sleep in the swing for over an hour in the late afternoon, and then sleep the whole night through. If your little one is fussing and crying around dinnertime, he might just be tired and in need of a nap. So, keep in mind that it's not always witching hour fussiness if crying begins at 4 p.m.

Indeed, there are many babies who could benefit a little nap around dinnertime. Trying to keep your child awake during this time is not only a difficult thing to do, but it could make things even more wearing on you. Don't suffer through every evening with a cranky and tired kid, simply because you think you'll be able to get him to sleep easier throughout the night. It doesn't work! You'll only wind up more frustrated in the long run if you try to keep your baby awake. You actually could wind up with a child who is so overtired that you won't be able to get him to sleep at all. So let him sleep if he's tired, especially during the witching hour.

Once your child is more than a couple months old, and has already established a fairly consistent sleeping pattern, you can begin to keep him awake in the evening. You can start to put your baby to bed earlier, and skip any late afternoon naps that might have wound up in the schedule. But until you reach that point, you should always let your child sleep when he needs to sleep.

CHAPTER REVIEW

Don't leave this chapter until you've mastered the following concepts:

1. Don't nurse, rock or drive your baby to sleep;
2. Get your sleep separation perfected; and
3. Learn how to cope with the witching hour;
   – and –
4. Learn how to put your baby to sleep awake.

Chapter 3

The Poison of the Pacifier

YOUR GOALS FOR THIS CHAPTER ARE:
1. Try your best to avoid a pacifier;
2. Understand the pitfalls of pacifiers;
   – and –
3. Learn how to pacify and then withdraw.

Before I get too far into how much I oppose a pacifier, allow me to say this: A pacifier with a *very limited* use during the first few weeks of your little one's life is okay. And yes, even *I* have fallen prey to the temptation and the ease of the dreaded pacifier. And believe me, it is a very tempting proposition, especially when you're completely exhausted and could really use a break.

The reason that a pacifier is so enticing is that during the first few weeks your newborn will want to suck on anything he can get his little lips around. You'll be tricked into thinking that your baby simply cannot be content unless he's sucking on something—that includes your breast, a finger, a pacifier, or a bottle. Your newborn's appetite to suck is virtually guaranteed to be voracious during the first couple weeks. Because your baby will be ever-so-happy when he's sucking, it is all too easy to fall prey to a pacifier. You just stick it in his mouth, and away you go to do whatever you want—take a shower—cook dinner—the sky is the limit when you stick that little thing in your kid's mouth.

The troubling aspect is that new parents find such a quick fix with a pacifier that they simply cannot stop using it. Parents and babies alike get completely addicted very fast. It's so incredibly easy to get hooked, and you'll both want to use it all the time. In reality, it's nothing more than a quick fix that you are guaranteed to pay dearly for later. You won't even realize that you're creating an obsessive pattern of behavior with your child that literally could take you years to reverse. Your baby (and you) will quickly become dependent on the poison of the pacifier and you will both want and need that little fix all day and night.

Admittedly, you can find plenty of parents out there who disagree with me on the pacifier issue.

And if you are among those who are inclined to join my cynics, then by all means use a pacifier to your heart's content. If you are not appalled by a three-year-old running around the grocery store with a pacifier stuck in his mouth, then this chapter probably isn't for you. Or if you are not going to mind getting up in the middle of the night for the next *year* of your little angel's life every time the pacifier pops out of his mouth, then skip this chapter for sure. You can still be successful with the Sleep Baby Sleep process if you choose to use a pacifier, but I can pretty much guarantee you that your results will not be nearly as fast or as painless.

In my opinion, your goal should not be to provide constant pacification to your baby; instead, it's much more beneficial to teach him how to pacify *himself.* If you empower your child with the ability to pacify himself—it's a gift that literally will last a lifetime. When your little one is sleeping or going to sleep, you don't want him rely on you or anything else to help him sleep. If you stick a pacifier in his mouth every time he needs to be soothed, then that's what you teach him to need every time. If you don't teach your child how to fall asleep on his own accord without being pacified in some form, then he'll always need something from you when he needs to sleep. You'll wind up with a child who needs you twenty-four hours a day—a situation that most parents cannot tolerate for any extended length of time.

If you enable your baby to get hooked on a pacifier, then until he is old enough to stick that thing in his mouth on his own, who do you think will be doing it...all night long? You guessed it— that would be you! *You* will be the one, for at least the first year or even more, to wake up each and every time that little devil pops out of your little angel's mouth. If you allow it, that little angel of yours will make sure that you have a permanent full-time position to soothe him in whatever way he needs and whenever he needs it, and that includes the graveyard shift with no over-time pay!

If you must use a pacifier, it should be used only as a stepping stone toward *self-pacification* and used only for the first few weeks of your baby's life. Use the pacifier as seldom as possible for as short amount of time as possible, in order to avoid getting your child totally reliant. Then, after your newborn is through the first couple of weeks, that raging desire of his to suck will diminish if you've use the pacifier at a complete minimum. On the other hand, if you've used the pacifier too much during the first couple weeks, then your infant's desire to suck will remain intense unless and until you break him of the addiction.

A pacifier should be viewed as any other form of soothing stimulus that you might use on your baby. If your child is fussing to the point of building into a cry, then let him have a pacifier, but keep it in his mouth only until he is has calmed down. Once he is quiet, take the pacifier out of his mouth. He might begin to fuss again, but don't stick it right back in. See if your little one can calm back down on his own. If not, try something else, like a rub on his little tummy or take him on a little tour around his new house.

You might just be pleasantly surprised to see what happens when you take the pacifier out of his mouth—your little one just might fall asleep on his own. On the flip side, if you keep the pacifier in his mouth for the rest of the night, then that's all he'll know. So, don't just shove a pacifier in your little angel's mouth for every little whimper. If you get into a habit of keeping one in his mouth all night, even if it's for just a couple of weeks, you can almost be guaranteed that your child will want that pacifier every night for a long time. Trust me, every *single* time he wakes up during each night, he'll expect and demand that pacifier.

By withdrawing the pacifier, consistently and over time, you will teach your little one to sleep without sucking. Remembering yet again that everything in this book is a *process* and nothing will happen immediately—just take your time to make things happen. If you take the pacifier out of your newborn's mouth and he freaks out and starts screaming, then stick it back in and try again next time. There is always next time. Keep trying and eventually, I promise you that when you pull out that pacifier one day, your little angel will just close his little eyes and actually will fall asleep without you.

Marcy's daughter wanted to suck on anything she could get those little lips around when she was first born. I warned Marcy not to overuse the pacifier, but she just couldn't help herself. She felt that her newborn couldn't be happy unless she had a pacifier in her mouth. The truth was, however, that Marcy had never even tried any other sort of soothing method, and the baby had quickly become addicted to the constant sucking.

Despite my admonitions, Marcy wound up using the pacifier all the time. Every time her little one would fuss, that thing was stuck right in her mouth. After about a month of this, her daughter couldn't calm down any other way unless she had the pacifier in her mouth. It seemed that nothing made Marcy's baby happy unless she had her little lips around that pacifier. As a mother, she hated the way it looked, but didn't think that there was any alternative.

I finally convinced Marcy that she did have a choice and that she could wean her baby off the pacifier. Luckily, since Marcy's little one was only six weeks when she began her attempt, the process proved quite easy. But until then, Marcy was sticking that pacifier back in her kid's mouth all day and night long, instead of getting her to calm down without it. When Marcy gave up the pacifier, she realized that there were so many other ways to pacify her little one. Both mother and child ended up much happier.

As I mentioned earlier, teaching your baby how to pacify himself will greatly decrease his constant need for you. If you are needed every single second of every single day, it will undoubtedly wear you down eventually. If instead you can at least get your child to not need you so much when it is time for him to sleep, then you can have just a little bit of air for yourself. So make sure you take care of yourself, and one of the ways to do that is by teaching your baby how to do just this one little thing without you—sleep!

CHAPTER REVIEW

(Don't move onto the next chapter until you understand the following concepts)

1. Understand the pitfalls of using a pacifier;
2. Treat the pacifier just like any other soothing stimulus;

– and –

3. Don't overuse the pacifier.

Chapter 4

To Crib or Not to Crib

YOUR GOALS FOR THIS CHAPTER ARE:

1. Get your baby out your room and into the crib;
2. Begin napping in the crib;

– and –

3. Develop bedtime and naptime rituals.

It is best to have your baby out of your room and into a crib as quickly as possible. As soon as your child is waking up only once or twice a night and is able to fall back to sleep on his own, he should be moved into a crib in his own room for the night. This typically will occur after you've been using the Sleep Baby Sleep process for about three to four weeks. If you're not yet comfortable with the idea of putting your little one in a crib, then wait until you and everybody in your household are ready. Remember that your ultimate objective is to separate yourself when it's time to sleep; and the sooner you begin, the sooner you will achieve your goal. So shoot for making the move to the crib as early as possible.

Putting your infant in a crib when he is young and still relatively unaware of his surroundings will allow for a smoother transition. When your child is about a month or two old, he will grow increasingly alert and will become more aware of his environment. If you make the change early enough so that he is not yet aware enough to even notice, then it will basically be a non-event. If you wait too long, your little one will be conscious of the transition; thus, the separation from you could be more difficult for everyone involved.

As mentioned earlier, it is best to move your child to a crib when he wakes only a couple times a night to feed and/or change *and* can fall back to sleep on his own relatively easily. If you still have to soothe your little one to get him back to sleep in the middle of the night, then you're probably not ready for the transfer to the crib. In that case, you should continue to use the bassinet technique for another couple weeks. If you put your little one in the crib too soon, you'll wind up in his room all night long trying to get him back to sleep.

Even if your baby is ready to move out of your room, *you* might not yet be psychologically prepared to make the separation. And that's okay! Your hormones might be raging and you might be having thoughts and feelings that you ordinarily wouldn't. You don't have to actually experience actual post-partum depression to feel a bit strange and off-kilter following childbirth. The emotional effects of these sweeping changes in your body can be enough to send you reeling for a while, not to mention the impact of radical lifestyle changes.

So, if you're feeling just a tad too hormonal to move your baby into a crib, wait until it feels right for you. A few weeks here or there in the grand scheme of things will not make a huge difference. If you follow the goals of the Sleep Baby Sleep process, you'll be there soon enough, so don't worry. Don't make things any harder for yourself than they already are, especially if you're feeling rather fragile. Be good to yourself—it's a challenging time for almost all who take the journey. So just wait until entire house is ready for the change.

If you started the sleep separation techniques since your child was born, then he should be ready for the transfer to a crib when he's around a month old. Some babies may take a little longer, no matter how hard you try, and some may take less. If you didn't begin the Sleep Baby Sleep method until your child was more than about four or five months old, then be sure to refer to Chapter 5 for details on dealing with older babies.

When you and your little one are ready, one good reason to get him out of your room is that by now your partner is probably good and ready to get some sleep again and is anxious for the midnight feedings to be somewhere other than in his room. Your partner may have even taken refuge in another room or on the living room couch by now, and you both might be feeling like it's time to try to have your life back in order. Although your partner should *absolutely* help you as much as you need for the first few weeks, you'll both notice a diminishing need for his assistance in the middle of the night.

I hate to sound like that submissive little housewife again, but once you get through the first few weeks there's really not much that your spouse can help you with at 3 a.m. You'll naturally find that you will need your partner's helping hand less and less in the middle of the night. Likewise, when your husband sees how little he is needed, he'll start to sleep right through your child's middle of the night feedings. Even my husband (who was an absolute saint when our boys were born) quickly realized after a few weeks that there wasn't much that he actually could help me with in the middle of the night. Also, I admittedly felt a tad guilty that he was waking up with me during the night since he had to wake up so early the next morning and go to work all day. So you may as well just let him sleep!

Of course, every relationship and every household is so very different, and if you feel that you want or need your spouse to stay involved in the middle of the night, by all means do it! Whatever works best for your family dynamics is what you should do. Do what's good for your life and for the relationships around you, and everything else will fall into place.

Remember that it's not only important for you to nurture your relationship with your child, but to be mindful of the relationship with your partner. It's all too easy to forget about anybody else's needs (including your own) when you are so wrapped up with the new baby. So, try to keep your *entire* house happy, and things will remain a lot more peaceful in the long run.

Ready for the crib. When you and your baby are ready for a crib, you'll be surprised at how easy the transition can be. You might want to have a monitor set up in your child's room (some of you might even have a video monitor set up), and you'll be able to listen intently to his every peep, but having nothing works just fine, too. If you do have a monitor, a great trick is to have the volume turned down to the lowest level. If the volume is turned to low, then you'll only hear the big noises instead of every little fuss or stir. If your baby is not too far from your room, then you might want to consider not having a monitor at all. That way, you will only tend to him when he is really fussing and needs you, and not reacting to every little peep.

I'll discuss nighttime rituals in greater detail later on, but your bedtime routine should pretty much stay the same as when your child was in the bassinet. I highly recommend getting a rocker or glider in your little one's room for nighttime feedings if it's feasible for you. A changing table, or even just a little changing "station" on the floor, in his room will also be very helpful. This way you can take care of everything in the middle of the night without even having to leave your baby's room.

You should do the final feeding of the night in the room in which the crib is located. The lights should be dim and the room nice and quiet. Try to avoid having any other activity going on around you. Have a night light set up in the baby's room so you can still see what you're doing in the middle of the night. Make sure that your little one has a full tummy, is burped and clean, and then put him down in the crib. If you have a security blanket, put it on your baby's chest. Once you put your child in the crib, you want to separate yourself as quickly as possible. Just give your baby a kiss and a few kind words, and then walk out of the room. (If your little one is more than a few months old, make sure you read Chapter 5 in conjunction with this chapter for tips on dealing with older babies.)

The first few nights with your child in the crib will probably be harder for you than it will be for him. Your hearing will suddenly become more acute than you ever thought possible. You will hear every little peep that comes out of that monitor, and you'll probably get less sleep than when your baby was right next to you. Even if your little angel has a huge stretch of sleep that first night in the crib, you're likely to be up most of the night with your ear pinned to the monitor waiting for that first peep out of him.

Your goal through the night is to only go into your child's room if the fussing begins to build into crying. The reason for this is simple: Even though it might sound like your child is going to start crying and screaming, he might suddenly be quiet again and fall back to sleep without you. What seems like a baby in need will turn out to be just a few moans and groans, and then he's back to sleep.

Also, you want to make your child work hard to get you back into the room. The harder you make him work for you, the quicker you will teach your baby that you will only return when you are needed. So make sure your child has a real need for you before you drag yourself out of bed. You'll notice more and more that your little one will wake up, fuss a bit, and then fall back to sleep.

In the beginning of this process, your baby may only fall back to sleep for a short time, and will then wake back up in another half-hour or so and be hungry or soiled. But at least you promoted a longer stretch of sleep and you've facilitated a little more sleep separation. You've taught your child that unless he needs you, he's on his own to sleep.

Over the next few weeks, the middle of the night feedings should grow to be fewer and farther between. Initially, you'll probably settle into a routine of getting up on two or three occasions around the same times each night for the next several weeks. You'll notice that your child will begin to stir right around the same time that you've been waking up to feed him. Don't just go in because you know it's time to feed your child. As the weeks go by, don't go back in to your baby's room unless he builds himself into an actual cry. You don't need to let him stay in his crib crying;

instead wait until your little one has just started crying and you are confident that he will not stop—then go in to feed him. Each and every time, you should make sure you are really needed before you even get out of bed.

If you follow this process, then your little one will begin to sleep right through one of his feedings, and then another, and then another—until your child completely sleeps through the night. So, don't just haul yourself out of bed in the middle of the night because it's the usual time that you feed your little angel. Make the stretches in between feedings farther and farther apart. Slowly over the next few weeks your baby will sleep more and more, and for longer stretches, until eventually one morning you'll joyfully wake up to realize that he just slept through the night!

Bedtime Rituals. An important part of helping your child to sleep through the night is to make sure you are into a solid bedtime routine. The hours before sleep should include plenty of love and attention. The evening should be a special time for the whole family, and should be as calm and quiet as possible (unless you have three wild boys, that is!) You might have a nightly bath, followed by reading in the rocker, or just some nice playtime on the floor.

Whatever your ritual is, it's very helpful to keep it fairly consistent before bedtime. If you do the same thing every night, it helps your child to understand that it is nearing bedtime and that it is therefore time for separation from you. The rituals can be whatever you choose and can be as long and as elaborate as you wish, as long as you make sure that you put your baby in the crib *awake*. Once your routine is complete, you give your little one a kiss goodnight and then leave the room.

Sleep gadgets. As part of the sleeping rituals in our home, each of our boys received their own little blanket when they were born (what we later called a "nanny"). Our boys to this day still sleep with their nannies and it provides a great amount of comfort to each of them. One of the smartest things I ever did was to buy two of the same nannies for each boy. That way if one got lost or needed to be cleaned, there was always another. And you wouldn't believe how many times over the years I have been ever so thankful to have that extra nanny on hand. A child can become quite dependent on a nanny, and being without one can definitely create a problem.

Creating an attachment to a security object, or nanny, is an excellent tool to help get a child sleeping independently. It's nice for your baby to have something important to him when he's trying to fall asleep alone, and getting him hooked on a nanny is the perfect way to do it. The easiest way to get your little one interested in a nanny is to have it with him all the time. Feeding, playing, walking, changing—just have it everywhere. Once your child develops an emotional attachment to the nanny, it will help him to feel more secure when you are not there.

Even as your baby matures, the security object will remain significant. You'll read later on that your little one might develop a certain degree of separation anxiety from you at around seven to ten months of age. This could happen even if your child has been sleeping through the night in his own room for many months. By having a special security object, the separation anxiety will be significantly reduced and will help your baby to feel less isolated without you.

A caveat: If you do decide to get your child interested in a security object, be it a blanket or stuffed animal or whatever, make sure that it is confined to your child's room by about two years of age. Nannies are not only very addictive, but they can be quite unsightly as well. Also, make it a rule to never let the nannies leave the house unless you're going on a trip, even when your child is young. Otherwise, the nanny is just another thing (like a pacifier...or a breast) to become too dependent upon. Just let the security object serve the limited purpose of aiding in sleep separation, and nothing more!

One great benefit to having a nanny is that your child can learn how to pacify himself *without needing you* every single time. So, it's a great tool— as long as you set the parameters from the beginning as to where and when the nanny will be used. Make sure that the usage of the nanny doesn't get out of hand, because it's all too easy to do. It's ever so easy to wind up with a two-year-old who demands to have his unsightly blanket with him everywhere he goes. Don't let your child demand anything from you, unless you *want* to give it. It's all up to you and it's all in your control.

Another great sleeping aid for your baby is a crib attachment. You can easily get by without one, but it can be a helpful tool in getting your child sleeping without you. If you go to a baby store, you'll see about a million different crib toys. Try to buy one that has lights and music and turns off automatically after 10 or 15 minutes. They even make some with remote controls now! I like the ones that have little movable things on them for your child to play with when he gets a little older. You should be able to firmly attach your crib toy to the side of the crib, and *always* be aware of any potential choking or suffocation hazards.

Get in the habit of turning the crib toy on every time you put your baby in the crib just before you walk out of the room. It not only serves as a good distraction from your departure, but it's a great cue for your little one to figure out that it's time to go to sleep. If your child starts to fuss after you've left the room, you can sneak back and turn it back on without even being noticed (hence, the new remote control versions). The lights and music are oft times mesmerizing and will help your angel fall back to sleep easier.

On the Road. Nannies and crib toys are also great for traveling. If you travel, you'll see that your baby won't be too thrilled about any changes in his sleeping environment, especially as he gets a little older. If you give your little angel his nanny and attach the familiar crib toy to wherever he is sleeping, he will feel much more secure and is certain to go to sleep with fewer objections even though you're on the road.

If your baby is still too young to be aware of his travels, then you will want to keep your routine as similar as possible. If your child is old enough to notice his new surroundings, it might take a little longer to get him sleeping than when you are at home. Like anything else, you should stick to your guns. If you get a few extra tears, do not placate your baby. Be firm and reassuring, and you will get your child where you want. We always traveled with a Pack-n-Play, and each of our children got used to it pretty quickly. It's a good idea to get one if you travel a lot, but it's easy to do without it. Just remember that if you want a flexible child, then create one! Don't let your travels, or anything for that matter, give you an excuse to have your baby wind up back in bed with you.

Napping in the Crib. If you're still working on the sleep separation and still teaching your infant to fall asleep without you, it's best to have him nap near you rather than away from you in a quiet room. Also, newborn naps are typically quite short and frequent, so it is easier to have your baby nearer to you since you'll have to tend to him more often.

When your infant is a little older, probably around two or three months old, you will notice that he will take longer naps, less often. Once your child has narrowed his naps down to two or three naps per day *and* is falling asleep without you, then it's a good time to start getting into the routine of napping him in the crib. If your little one is more than five or six months old, be sure to read Chapter 5 for more detail on what to do with older babies.

Rituals for napping in the crib are useful, but it's best to keep them to a minimum during the day. I always liked skipping the reading, etcetera, during the day so that my little one could go right to sleep. Then you will eventually be able to just put your little one down for a nap with a quick kiss and have some time to yourself during the day. Save the extravagant routines for the nighttime. On the other hand, you may like reading or playing on the floor before a nap—it's all up to you. No matter what your rituals are, putting your child in the crib while he's awake is your mission.

You also want to make sure your baby has a full tummy when he goes down for a nap. This way you can avoid a nap being cut short due to hunger. But don't nurse your child to sleep for his naps! You must resist the ease of nursing your little angel to sleep every time—it will be your downfall.

If you have your baby on a good napping routine, he will probably begin to nap only twice a day at around four to six months old. It depends on your particular child, but the naps will probably be mid-morning, and then early afternoon. When your child is about a year old—and hopefully not sooner—he will probably go down to one early afternoon nap for a couple of hours.

I highly recommend getting your child on a regular nap routine once his naps become fairly predictable. Enforcing naps at a scheduled time every day as your baby matures is very helpful. First of all, if you don't teach him to nap, I can promise you that you *will* have a tired and cranky kid on your hands. And don't underestimate the strain that a chronically exhausted kid and an overstressed mommy can have on a household. Secondly, insisting on the naps will help you to find the time that you need for yourself. It's very rejuvenating to be able to get a couple (or even a few) hours to yourself during the day. So, insist on the naps. Remember—you can create what you want!

As a side note, if your child is in daycare and you are not together during the day, then the daytime nap scene is for the most part out of your control. If at all possible, let your daycare provider know how and when you would like your baby to nap. You might not have any control over the situation, but if you do, make sure to guide your provider to napping your child the way you want him napped.

In the event that you simply have absolutely no control over the daytime naps, then your efforts to have your baby's sleeping habits in order will just have to be done at night. But regardless of what your daytime life situation is, with diligence you will have your little one sleeping through the night in no time.

CHAPTER REVIEW

(Don't move onto the next chapter until you understand the following concepts)

1. Is your baby ready to move into a crib?
2. Start napping in the crib;

                    – and –

3. Understand the importance of rituals and routines at bedtime.

Chapter 5

It's Never Too Late to Begin

This chapter is dedicated specifically to those of you who are getting somewhat of a later start on the Sleep Baby Sleep method. You should familiarize yourself with the rest of the book before reading this chapter, because it all works together. If your baby is still young enough to have benefited from my ideas so far, then you could skip this chapter altogether; however, this chapter can be useful for any parent as it serves as a review of the Sleep Baby Sleep concepts, and more importantly discusses child rearing in general. So, read it if you have the time.

YOUR GOALS FOR THIS CHAPTER ARE:

1. Make the commitment to yourself that you *will* get your baby sleeping through the night without you;
2. Get your child interested in a security object;
3. Develop a consistent night time ritual *after* you feed your baby;
4. Put your baby to sleep awake;

– and –

5. Get your baby to fall asleep independently.

So, here you are. Your child is now five, ten, twelve months, or even older, and you are *exhausted.* You're still up several times during each night, if not more, and your baby cannot fall asleep without you. You might be nursing your little one on demand around the clock, and/or rocking your baby for an hour or more just to get him to sleep at night. You have virtually not a minute of privacy or downtime, and it's starting to get to you. You have, for all intents and purposes, turned into...yes...a "Debbie"! Luckily enough though, you've found this book and you and you have the ammunition to begin to unravel what has turned into quite an exhausting and frustrating venture for you.

Your first step is to make the decision that you are ready to implement some changes in your house. Undoing the patterns that have developed between your baby and you will almost inevitably produce significant stress and anxiety initially for both of you, and you need to be prepared for a lot of tears for the next couple of weeks.

It may be that you simply are not yet ready to make your child cry in order to achieve these changes. It all depends on you and your particular level of tolerance for your situation. Some parents can put up with lack of sleep for years, but others (like me) cannot.

You might have noticed that your child is starting to rule your house. He may have become demanding and completely reliant on you for *everything*, and you probably don't get a second to yourself. If you simply do not want to put up with (or cannot tolerate another minute of) this anymore, then you are probably ready to let your little one cry it out for the next couple of weeks to achieve your goal of getting him sleeping on his own.

There are a couple of things that you need to keep in mind when making your decision whether to suffer through the next couple of weeks to make some changes: First of all, the only way to have your baby sleeping without you once such deeply imbedded behavior patterns have developed is to force him to cry through it until your imposed upon changes are accepted. Your child has grown accustomed to expecting certain things from you, and is not likely to give up those expectations without a fight. Unfortunately, there is just no other way when you have an older baby. Simply put: There is no "miracle cure". There will be a couple weeks of serious crying before you can get your angel sleeping through the night, and there's no way around it. (With your next baby, you can start from the beginning and not have to deal with the crying.)

The other important thing you need to understand is that if you don't make changes now, you are likely to be dealing with lack of sleep and lack of privacy for many years to come. If you accept this, and your spouse completely supports you in your decision, well then more power to you. But if you're like most people, your situation has probably become intolerable and you need to make some changes.

There's even more to it than that. As I've mentioned before, if you want to raise a disciplined and respectful child, you cannot be an indulgent parent. Don't let your child rule any part of his life (or yours!), whether it be sleeping, eating, toy playing, or whatever. You are the adult and you make the decisions. It is *not* a democracy, and allowing your child to think that it is will only lead to bigger and bigger problems.

By the time your child is three, he will completely boss your house, and it will only get worse from there. Catering to your little angel incessantly and giving in to his every want and whim will *not* make you a better parent, and more importantly will not make him a better person. The truth of the matter is that if you set boundaries for your child, and enforce your rules with positive reinforcement and consequences, you will empower your child to develop into a healthier, better adjusted person. In other words, you actually are contributing to your offspring's emotional well-being by being firm and defining limits.

The fact that you are strict doesn't exclude you from being a loving, tender parent. I am one of the strictest for sure, but am undoubtedly one of the most tender and nurturing parents that I know. I constantly work to boost my boys' self-esteem, and always strive to make each one of them feel great about themselves. But, make no mistake: *I am tough!* The rules in my house are clearly defined, as are the consequences for bad behavior. If you think about it—sleeping is only one aspect of the whole picture. Keep that in mind as you raise your children and as you try to keep order in your house.

Things Need to Change. No matter how difficult it will be for you to make some changes, you know that it's necessary in order for you to have your life back. You know that you are now so over-tired that you're thinking that you have become a different person altogether. You are giving in to your baby way too much, and he is beginning to rule your house. So, it's time. It's time to change the patterns of behavior, because if you don't do it now—you'll regret it. Do it now and struggle for the next few weeks, and you'll have your life back and your child where you want.

You can still be an amazing parent even though your baby is not sleeping with you. You can still be kind and loving even though you're about to let your child cry it out for the next couple of weeks, and don't forget that. If you don't do it now, it could literally take you *years* to get your child sleeping independently. You shouldn't have to wait years to have your life (and your bed) back—that's not what parenting is all about.

I am well aware that it is a very difficult decision for you to force these changes on your poor defenseless little angel. No mother wants to make their child unhappy, but it is the only way you can get him to sleep without you. You need to remember, however, that the changes that you are about to impose will make your child happier when it's all over.

I am willing to bet that your baby doesn't wake up happy, and in fact probably spends most of his day being cranky, demanding and tired. This is because your baby cannot get a good night's sleep or a good nap, especially if it takes you an hour or more just to get him sleeping. *That kid is as tired as you are!* He's up all night, too.

Although you might think that you are making your angel miserable by instituting these changes, you will definitely have a happier child when it's over. Your baby will have happier days, and will not be so needy and agitated all the time. So when you are making the commitment to let your little one scream and cry for the next couple of weeks, remember that you are doing it for both of you, and it is not merely a selfish act on your behalf.

<u>Easing the Transition.</u> Though undoing established patterns will undoubtedly pose a challenge for everyone under your roof, there are several preliminary steps that you can take to make your upcoming transition a bit easier for you all. The first thing you can do is to get your child interested a security object. A security object, or a "nanny" as I call it, is a great technique to help prepare your little one for the upcoming changes, thereby alleviating at least some of the stress involved in getting him to sleep without you.

Your child may already have an object that has become his nanny. If he has, then your transition will be all the easier (but by no stretch of the imagination will it be easy). If not, then it's time to start. Look around your house, and pick a soft, small blanket or stuffed animal, one that your child might already be keen on. Anything you or your baby chooses will be fine, but just be *extremely* careful of any potential choking or suffocation hazard. You don't want to use anything for a nanny that poses any kind of danger for your baby. If you don't have anything around the house that works, then go buy a small, soft blanket to use as a nanny.

The best way to get your child interested in the nanny is to make sure that you keep it everywhere that he is, all the time. When you're reading a story, have the nanny on his lap; when your baby goes to sleep—put the nanny on him or next to him; when you're nursing—let the nanny be on his tummy or in his hands. Just let it be everywhere, every day, all the time. You'll be pleasantly surprised at how quickly your little one will become attached to this inanimate object. You will probably notice a strong desire for the nanny beginning to develop within the first couple of weeks of introducing the object.

Establishing the security object enables a child to feel more secure when he is left to sleep on his own. Your little one has completely grown accustomed to your presence when he falls asleep. Now that you are going to make a separation from those sleeping episodes, he is likely at first to feel insecure and uncomfortable without having you there. Having a nanny that gives your child some security independent from you will make the separation easier to cope with, and will make it a less stressful event for everyone involved. Hence, the term security object. The nanny empowers your child to feel comfortable about sleeping without mommy's constant pacification and proximity.

Bedtime Rituals a Must. A solid bedtime routine is another important aspect to getting your baby to sleep through the night, and can help to alleviate the new stress of sleeping without mommy. The more of a routine that you have in place, the quicker your little one will grow accustomed to your departure at the close of that routine. Once you begin to separate from your child on a nightly basis, it will be only a matter of a couple of weeks for him to understand that when the routine is over—you are leaving and he is on his own to sleep. Most children thrive on routine. The more consistent you are with your child, the faster he will grow to accept your new behavior as a fact of life. And this will be true no matter how much resistance he shows at first.

By now, you probably have at least some sort of bedtime routine going. If not, then now is a good time to start. Try to have the majority of your bedtime routine occur in the child's bedroom. Even if you're not quite ready to put your little one in his own room, you should at least get him used to spending time there before bed. Spend at least a half-hour or so on a nighttime ritual (especially if your baby is more than six months old), and make sure you do your best to keep the routine fairly consistent each night. A typical routine includes feeding your child, a nice warm bath, followed by some playtime, then closing with a book or two. You can do whatever routine you like, so long as you are sure to maintain consistency and vow to never feed your baby last. You'll figure out soon enough what is a good routine for your child and you. A routine that works well for one family might not always work well for another, so be sure to figure out what works best in your situation.

Jodi and her husband had a routine of playing on the floor for a while with their new daughter. The playing was then followed by a warm bath, and then they put their baby in the crib for bed, and left the room. Even though they had stuck with this routine fairly consistently for several weeks, their little one had trouble falling asleep each night once she was put in her crib. Jodi began to think that the bath was stimulating her daughter too much, so they decided to switch the routine around and give her a bath before feeding and playing. Jodi's intuition was correct. As soon as they started giving the baby a bath in the beginning of the routine instead of at the end, she fell asleep much faster. It was just that little change in the routine that was enough to make their daughter more relaxed and able to fall asleep. So, figure out what works well for your family, follow your intuition, and then just stick with it each night.

If you have an older baby, you should always feed him at the start of your nighttime ritual. If you're just starting the Sleep Baby Sleep technique with a child who is used to being nursed or rocked to sleep, you both need to rid yourselves of the notion that feeding and sleeping go hand-in-hand. Start feeding your child *before* the bath, the playing, and the books, and rid yourself of the old bad habit of nursing or rocking him to sleep. This is the key to the Sleep Baby Sleep technique. You must teach your little one how to sleep without you if you want him to sleep through the night. You will not—I repeat, *will not* be able to teach your baby how to fall asleep without you if you nurse or rock him to sleep every day and night. There's just no way. It won't be an easy task to make this change, but do it now and you'll be forever thankful that you did. Make the commitment that as part of your new bedtime routine, you will not nurse or rock your little one to sleep. You will feed your child in the *beginning* of the routine—end never at the end. No ifs, ands, or buts!

Another helpful way to ease the stress of the transition is to have a crib toy attached to the crib that turns off automatically after a few minutes. As mentioned in another chapter, there are scores of varieties of crib toys. Just make sure that if you do get one, that it has sounds and lights, and turns off automatically. The most effective way to use the crib toy as part of your bedtime routine is to turn it on just before you leave the room for the night. It not only serves as an excellent distraction for your departure, but it also gives your child the signal that it is time for you to leave and for him to sleep alone. If you don't have or don't want to get a crib toy, it's not by any stretch of the imagination a fatal omission. It's just one more thing that can assist you in attaining your goal.

Although you can do all of these things to help ease your baby into sleeping alone, you need to understand that no matter how well you prepare, the evolution will not happen overnight. Like everything else throughout the book, this too is a process. You have gotten yourself into a routine with your child, and no matter how much you don't like it, it is going to take some time to undo. You're probably looking at least two to three weeks of very hard work before your little one is sleeping soundly in his own crib. But if you're committed to getting your baby to sleep without you, you *can* and *will* do this.

When you start, you should prepare yourself for the first week to be virtually sleepless. The beginning will be the most challenging part of the transition. Just a few sleepless nights for the first week, followed by another couple weeks of difficult nights, and then you'll be there! Hold firm to your ground for three weeks, or maybe four at the most, and that little baby who has been keeping you up for months on end will *finally* be sleeping through the night. Keep the end in sight and stay focused, and it will happen—but remember, it's a process!

Jane's ten month old was not even close to sleeping through the night when she finally decided to implement the Sleep Baby Sleep technique. Jane was extremely exhausted from having her little girl in bed with them since birth, and she did not think it was possible to get her baby into a crib. Her daughter had only rarely fallen asleep without being nursed or rocked, and had never once napped alone in the entire ten months. The only time her baby had ever taken a nap was when Jane was in bed with her while she slept.

Jane took a couple weeks to prepare for the big event of getting her daughter sleeping alone, and understanding that these changes would not happen overnight was very helpful. Mommy got a good game plan together and gave herself a start date, and reminded herself all along that it would take at least a few weeks of torture to get to where she wanted—and needed—to be. She prepared herself for the challenge, and when the target day came she implemented the plan and began to separate from her baby for sleep times.

After what felt like a barbaric first week, Jane finally saw some real progress. Even though she could really notice the differences, she was so exhausted that she almost gave in and let her daughter back in their bed. Instead Jane kept with it, and by the end of the third week her little girl slept peacefully in the crib. Her daughter even began napping on her own, which is something that

Jane thought could never happen. To this day, Jane cannot believe how short of a time it took to make such major changes in their house. What seemed like a monumental transition turned out to be so minor in the scheme of things, and everybody in the house was so much happier when it was finally over.

Jane is a perfect example of how determination and will can turn things around in a very short period of time. She knew that she wanted and needed her baby out of her bed and sleeping through the night. She knew that her relationship with her husband was suffering and that she was chronically tired and cranky. She needed to have her life back. Jane set her mind to it, gave herself a time frame, and then just made the changes happen. You, too, have the power to institute these changes if you put your mind to it, and don't think for a moment that you are not in total control of your situation! It's time for you to get your life back, too. *You* are in the driver's seat and don't you forget it!

Daytime Techniques. If you haven't gone back to work yet, the daytime is also a great time to apply the sleep separation techniques. You should work both day and night to accomplish your goals, especially if you want your sleeping problems behind you as quickly as possible. So, in conjunction with having your child sleeping in his crib at night, you should have him take naps in there as well. Although you are going to be exhausted during this short stretch of retraining your child, it's important that you apply the process around the clock.

Don't nap your little one in the crib during the day, and then let him sleep in your bed all night long, or visa versa. Maintain consistency while teaching your baby how to sleep without you, and keep the sleeping rituals consistent twenty-four hours a day. This is the way for you to achieve your mission as quickly as possible with the least amount of stress in your house.

If you have been nursing your child on demand and/or nursing him to sleep each time, then you are going to need to put him on a daytime feeding schedule before you get started. Chapters 2 and 8 can help you get started on a good schedule, so refer to those sections if you need to. Though it might seem a little late in the game to start your child on a feeding schedule, the real purpose for it is to force you to move away from allowing yourself to be used as a human pacifier.

Here's a little secret: Mothers who nurse on demand around the clock *do not* have children who sleep without them. You need to nurse your child *only* when he is actually hungry and needs to eat, and *stop* nursing him if he needs help falling asleep or wants to be pacified. Limiting your nursing to only when it is time to eat will force you (and your child) to figure out how to be pacified in other ways when it's not feeding time. I know you may not believe me, but there are other ways to pacify your little one, and you and your baby need to learn what they are; otherwise, you'll maintain this status as human pacifier for many months, and maybe even years to come.

At this point, you probably cannot even imagine anything other than your breast that can quiet down your child, but it's out there, I promise you. If your baby is fussy when it's not time to feed him, try to think of some other way to pacify him other than your breast. Take that little angel for a walk, give him a toy, or sing him a song. You could try different positions, different music, or different rooms. Just make the commitment to yourself that you will no longer use your breast unless your child is hungry, and you'll get through it.

Trust your intuition, *and use it*. I promise you those maternal instincts are stronger than you think. After a couple weeks of what will seem like torture, you'll begin to figure out alternative soothing techniques to quiet your little one down. The bad news is that it won't happen overnight. Just make that commitment that your breasts will not be on the list of things to calm your child down, and you'll be all the closer to accomplishing your goal of getting him to sleep alone.

So, get your baby on a feeding schedule during the day, and it will help to prepare you for the night time challenge. It might seem too overwhelming for you to make these daytime changes while simultaneously trying to have your child sleeping a crib at night, but it's best to do it all at once. Make your changes in a planned and methodical manner, and you'll accomplish your goals quickly.

Honey, it's time (to get your child sleeping without you)! As mentioned earlier, your first step has to be making the commitment to yourself that you will *never* again nurse or rock your child to sleep (except on special occasions like traveling or illness). If you are not ready to make this agreement with yourself, then you are simply not ready to begin. You need to be mentally prepared to make the separation, and if you're not, then just wait longer. Although it takes no more than a few weeks, you need to be completely at peace with the struggles that you are about to embark upon; otherwise, you just won't be able to do it. Your personal commitment needs to be established before you do anything else.

When you're emotionally committed to make some changes, your next step is to get together a game plan for getting your child sleeping without you. Plan it out a week or so in advance, and have everything in place and thought out before you begin. The last thing you want to do is go down this new road in a haphazard manner without a clearly defined map of where you want to be.

While you're planning out your strategies, you should simultaneously work on getting your little one interested in a security object. At the same time, make sure you get a good nighttime routine in place. Do this for a couple weeks if you want before you actually begin your sleep separation efforts. There's no huge hurry now since you've already waited this long, and a couple of weeks of contemplation and preparation will probably suit you well.

Once you're ready to begin, remember to start your new nighttime routine by feeding, then afterward complete whatever other rituals that you have. *Don't feed your child last!* When your little one is fed, clean and your routine is complete, then put him in the crib while he is still awake. Give your child his little nanny, turn on the crib toy (if you have one), and then give him a kiss goodnight. Once you plant that kiss on your baby's cheek, turn around and head for the door without looking back.

Rest assured that your child *will* resist your new maneuvers and will probably start screaming his little head off. Imagine his shock and disbelief as you turn to walk out of the room for that very first time. You can count on the fact that your little one is going let you know how truly unhappy he is about this new predicament that you have gotten him into.

He Can Cry If He Wants To. Crying is almost guaranteed to be part of your child's new repertoire over the next week or two, so prepare yourself and remember to forge ahead and not lose sight of your goals. When your child does start to cry because you've left the room, do not go back in. Instead, see if he can calm down without you. I need to warn you though: In all likelihood, that little angel of yours will do nothing of the sort.

When your baby doesn't quiet down and continues to cry, you should put yourself on a schedule for returning to his room. At first, you'll want your return intervals set at about five or ten minutes. In other words, just watch the clock and do not go back in until you have reached the end of the scheduled time.

Once you survive through that first five or ten minutes, then go back into the room if your baby is still crying. You should go in only for a very brief moment to offer a few kind words of reassurance and to give your child a little pat on the tummy. *Do not pick your baby up!* If he has pulled himself up, gently lay him back down, turn on the crib toy, and put his nanny on his chest. Then leave.

Do not expect your child to be calm when you walk out of his room again. In fact, during the first week of this, he will probably cry all the harder upon your departure. But you nonetheless need to leave. You need to teach your baby *right now* that he needs to sleep by himself. (You are also teaching your little angel that his tantrums won't work. Giving in only reinforces his behavior, which could turn into a rod in your back for a long time.)

So, even though your poor little baby is crying, you have to leave the room. See if he can either calm down on his own or simply fall asleep crying. If your child doesn't stop crying by the end of another five or ten minutes (which he probably won't), then briefly go back into his room to reassure him. Make each return interval a little longer than the time before. Remember that your sole purpose for going back into his room is to let him know that you are there if he *needs* you and that you have not deserted him. Don't do one thing other than to reassure your child for a few brief seconds, and then leave.

Although this will be a very difficult time for

everyone involved, understand that things will begin to get easier within about a week. But in the beginning, have absolutely no expectation that you will be able to console your little one when you go into his room. Your child wants nothing more from you than what he's gotten all along up until now, and is not going to be happy when he doesn't get it. No matter what you do at this point, your little bundle of joy (or should I say: your bundle of misery) is going to be completely frustrated over this sudden change.

Your baby at some point during the night will either fall asleep (yes, without you!) or will calm down on his own. Continue to increase the intervals as the days go on. By the second night, you should be going back in every fifteen or twenty minutes, but only if he's crying. On night three, your returns should be no less than thirty minutes apart. At the week's end, the intervals should be forty-five minutes apart (although most of you by then will have your child sleeping with just twenty or thirty minute intervals).

I'm well aware that it is going to be *extremely* difficult for you to be on the other side of that door listening to your poor baby screaming for you. It is tough situation to tolerate, I know. Every inch of you will want to rescue your child from his misery, but at the same time you will know deep down that you're doing the right thing. Just stick to your time intervals, let your child know you haven't abandoned him, and you will begin to teach him how to sleep without you.

While you're watching the clock outside your child's room, you will suddenly realize that the crying has stopped and your child has either calmed down or has fallen asleep. Be prepared though, because it might literally take you hours the first night to get your baby sleeping. Adding insult to injury, when you do finally get him to sleep, he might only sleep for an hour or so before he awakes to find himself alone, and the whole process will begin again. The good news is that as each day passes, your baby will fall asleep faster and faster.

Within a week or two, your baby will probably only cry for a few minutes and then will fall right to sleep on his own. After three or four weeks, your little one probably won't even shed a tear when you kiss him goodnight, *and* will then sleep the whole night through. Although you might not believe this now, your baby will quickly adapt to his new parameters if you stick to your guns. You'll see that he will actually begin to calm himself down, rather than always needing you to do it for him. You'll have your own life back, and have a happier and less demanding baby who sleeps regularly and is finally well-rested. The payoff for the torture you're about to put yourself through is tremendous—so just do it and get it over with!

Nix the nighttime feedings. An important part of getting your child to sleep through the night is to stop his feedings throughout the night. If your older baby is not yet sleeping through the night, he is probably waking up numerous times demanding to be nursed until he falls back to sleep. If you have a normal, healthy baby who is older than four months old, he in all likelihood doesn't need to be fed. It's more probable that he wakes up, but needs you to pacify him to go back to sleep. So, even though your little one doesn't *need* to feed anymore, you've found yourself in this exhausting pattern of nursing your baby throughout the night just to get him back to sleep.

Part of your new regimen needs to be to work toward completely weaning your child off of the middle of the night feedings. You can do it gradually, or you can just go cold turkey and get it over with quickly. If you feel like you can cut out all of them at once, then you should try. But most moms feel more comfortable cutting down to one or two feedings a night for the first week or so, and then gradually eliminating the remaining feedings over the course of the next several weeks. The goal is that by the time you have your baby falling asleep without you (within two or three weeks), he will also be forgetting about your breasts at 3 a.m. So, once he can fall asleep on his own, he won't be waking up in the middle of the night crying for you.

If you're going to take it slowly, then pick one or two designated feeding times during the night. Feed your child *only* on those selected times. When he wakes up and it is not a chosen feeding time, don't go into his room right away. Give a time period for your baby to cry and then go into the room to soothe him, but do not take him out of the crib. I know it might seem impossible at first to accomplish this, but you *will* be able cut out any particular feeding by the week's end. Make the promise to yourself that you will no longer console with your breast, a bottle or rocking (except on special occasions). Your child is now old enough to respond to other forms of soothing, and nursing him to quiet him down in the middle of the night is *not* the only option.

Sometimes you might have trouble eliminating one of the night feedings. Either your child is putting up too much of a fight or you are just not ready to give it up altogether. In that event, you'll have to ease your baby into the change instead of getting rid of it quickly. Rather than nursing for a full twenty or thirty minutes, try giving your child only a couple minutes of your breast. Don't let it be a full nursing session. At the same time you want to make him really work to get you back in the room for that particular session. Don't go into your little one's room with the first peep that you hear. When you do finally go in and only give him a teeny bit, your child will begin to realize that it is not worth all that crying to only get a couple minutes of your breasts.

As mentioned earlier, a few tears at this point should never be enough to get you back into your child's room, unless of course you think that something is wrong. Just like when you are trying to get your baby to sleep, give yourself a certain number of minutes for your child to cry, and then go console him. As the time intervals grow longer as the days go by, you'll notice that he will begin to soothe himself back to sleep without you.

It won't take long for your baby to figure out that it simply takes too much effort to get you into his room at 2 a.m., especially if he gets nothing to eat and you only stay for a few brief seconds. Your child will naturally begin to wake up less and less during the night, and will quickly learn how to comfort himself more and more. Soon you'll notice that when your baby wakes up in the middle of night (which almost all babies do), he won't even cry out for you, and will only fuss for a few minutes and then put *himself* back to sleep. Sooner than you can even believe, you *all* will be sleeping through the night and you will have your life back!

Sarah's daughter, Amy, is great example of how quickly an older baby can respond to the Sleep Baby Sleep method. Sarah didn't begin using the Sleep Baby Sleep method until Amy was nine months old. Her daughter spent her first two or three months sleeping in between mommy and daddy, and basically nursed on demand twenty-four hours a day. After a few months of this, Sarah decided that it was time to get Amy into a crib, so they set up a crib for her in their bedroom. After Amy was nursed to sleep, Sarah would put her into the crib and there she would sleep soundly until about 1 a.m. Each night when the baby would stir, Sarah would bring the baby into their bed and nurse her back to sleep. It was only when her daughter was fast asleep that Sarah would return her to the crib. Then, usually once an hour after that, Amy would stir and the pattern would repeat itself: Sarah would bring her little girl back into their bed, nurse her back to sleep, and then put her back into the crib.

This pattern went on for many months. Amy needed her mother in order to fall back to sleep each and every time she awoke, and had never learned how to fall asleep on her own. Sarah grew increasingly exhausted and eventually gave up on even trying to put Amy back into the crib after each feeding. After all, she knew her baby would be waking up again shortly, so what was the point of even trying to get her back in the crib? Out of sheer exhaustion, Sarah would just let Amy stay in her bed from 1 a.m. until morning. Even though the initial attempt was made to separate herself from her daughter, Sarah wound up nursing around the clock. At nine months, their little angel was not even close to sleeping through the night.

When Sarah came to me, she had made the commitment in her mind that changes were immediately necessary. Though her daughter was already nine months old when Sarah began the Sleep Baby Sleep process, it didn't take long at all to get Amy into her own crib and sleeping independently. In fact, that little angel was sleeping through the night before she turned eleven months—just four weeks after Sarah began the process!

The first few weeks were the hardest, and Sarah was initially more exhausted than when she was nursing her little one around the clock. But Sarah was completely committed to getting her daughter out of their bed. It was a grueling couple of weeks, but then it wasn't long at all that mom and dad had their bed back, and more importantly their privacy back.

The whole house slept through the night (most of the nights thereafter), and everyone was much happier.

Sarah is the perfect example that if you have the dedication to struggle through only a couple of weeks, your child can be sleeping through the night. Make the commitment *now* to have your baby sleeping on his own and through the night, and it can and will happen. Not only will you get your life back, but your child will begin to sleep better and longer. Once your child starts sleeping better, he will wake up happier and better rested, and he won't be as needy and agitated while he's awake. Remember, the changes are for all of you! Everyone in your house needs to sleep better, and *now* is the time to make it happen.

CHAPTER REVIEW

(Don't move onto the next chapter until you've mastered the following concepts)

1. Mentally prepare for the journey you are about to embark upon;
2. Develop a well thought out strategy;
3. Get your child interested in a security object;
4. Stop nursing on demand;

– and –

5. Eliminate the nighttime feedings

Chapter 6

Taking It Into Toddlerhood

YOUR GOALS FOR THIS CHAPTER ARE:

1. Overcoming toddler sleep issues;

– and –

2. Coping with nighttime terrors.

E veryone under your roof will reap the benefits if you've followed the Sleep Baby Sleep philosophy as your baby matures into a toddler. You will notice how happy and alert your child is as he grows. Your little one will nap regularly and sleep in his own space, and will wake up a joy (most of the time, that is). Your child will be sleeping undisturbed fairly consistently, and putting himself back to sleep in the middle of the night when he awakes.

You (and your spouse) will be happier, too. Your child will sleep when you want him to, while you find time for yourself during his naps and plenty of privacy at night. You'll see how dramatically different your life is compared to your friends who never got their kids sleeping without them. Every part of your life will be easier and everyone will get some good shut-eye.

That's the good news. The bad news is that no matter how well your child has been sleeping, you are bound to run into periodic resistance with getting and/or keeping him asleep. So, long after that little angel has achieved champion sleeper status, you will come across some degree of protest when you go to put him to sleep one night.

These attempted coups can present even more of a challenge than when your child was younger. Now, he is more aware of his surroundings and has gotten a real sense of his ability to control his environment. The word "no" has probably become one of his absolute favorites. Challenging you and your rules is a normal part of your child's development. These uprisings need to be handled strictly, and you *cannot* give in to your little one's demands. Remember, this is not a democracy and you make the rules (look to Chapter 5 to help you with this).

Barbara's nine month old daughter had been sleeping through the night since she was ten weeks old. Barbara thought she had it made through the tough part. Her little one had been going to sleep like the dream child and Barbara hardly ever had to go into her daughter's room in the middle of the night. All of the sudden, one night, the daughter began screaming after mommy kissed her goodnight. She had never objected before to Barbara's departure, so the first instinct was to pick her baby back up to see what was wrong. As soon as she picked her daughter up, the crying stopped. Barbara noted that her daughter had no fever, nor any other sign of sickness. After fully assessing the situation, she determined there was absolutely nothing wrong with her child, and that she simply wanted to be picked back up. So Barbara put her back into the crib, but again the baby screamed when mommy tried to leave. This time the crying was even louder.

If there ever is an appropriate time for you to let your child cry it out, well then this is it. If you keep going back into his room after you've made certain that your baby is not ill and doesn't need you for anything, then you will very quickly—and I mean *very* quickly—condition him to understand how very simple it is to get you back in his room.

Toddlers *love* to control any part of their environment that they possibly can. If you let your little one see that he is suddenly able to be in charge of the bedtime scene, then you will run into trouble faster than you can ever believe. So, if you're confident that nothing is wrong, even if your child is crying and sad—don't be fooled by the attempted coup and just turn around and leave.

Unfortunately, you might have to let your child cry for twenty to thirty minutes until he falls back to sleep. And even though you may have never had to make him cry it out before, you're going to have to do it now if you want to nip any sleeping issues in the bud. If it's killing you to let him cry, look at the clock and promise yourself that you won't go back in until a certain time. If you get to that time and he's still screaming, then go into his room, but as always, *don't take him out of the crib.* If you're certain your child doesn't need anything, just go in to let him know he's okay and secure, give him a quick pat and then leave.

Don't stay with your child even if he's still crying. Once you leave the room, go back on the clock. It probably won't take more than couple episodes of this to cure him for good, and your child will be back to sleeping soundly once again. On the other hand, if you succumb to his demands at this stage of the game, then it seriously, could take *months* to repair what developed in just a few nights.

The longer you allow your toddler to be conditioned (or should I say that he conditions you!), the longer it will take you to have him sleeping through the night again. If you're not careful, your little one could even wind up back in bed with you. Your child will get through this little opposition phase quickly if you handle it swiftly and with control.

If you started the Sleep Baby Sleep technique with a newborn, you probably have not had to make him cry it out until now. That makes this sudden change even more challenging to cope with. Even though this phase could be most taxing on you, keep in mind that it is best for your child and you to maintain sleep separation through toddlerhood. You need your sleep and your private time, and you don't want to start giving it up at this point.

Some children never go through any toddler opposition periods at all. If you're one of the lucky ones with a completely compliant angel, then just keep plugging away with what you're doing. But if you're not, hopefully I've given you enough ammunition to confront the situation and deal with it speedily in order to keep things from getting out of hand.

Baby Pull-ups. When your child first figures out how to pull himself up in the crib, it's so very delightful. You'll come into his room one bright and sunny morning to see that adorable little face peering over the crib bars with a huge smile on his face. First thing in the morning, yes, it's wonderful; but in the middle of the night, when the young acrobat can't figure out how to lie back down and is screaming his head off, it's quite a different story and not nearly as attractive.

The problem is that most babies learn how to pull themselves up before they can figure out how to lay themselves back down. So, long after your child is sleeping through the night, this inability to lie back down is likely to present a bit of a glitch in your blissful, uninterrupted nights. One night, out of nowhere, you'll hear your baby screaming. You'll go to check on him only to find him clinging to the side of the crib. He will be exhausted and desperate for sleep, but unable to figure out how to simply lie back down.

What you need to do in this case is to quietly lay him right back down—and then leave. Don't talk to your child or stimulate him in any way. Just give him a little pat on the tummy, give him his nanny, and make for the door. If he cries when you leave, just keep right on walking.

You might find that it happens all over again ten minutes later. Just keep returning to the room, quickly lay your child back down, and leave. He will catch on very quickly, and within a day or two will probably figure out how to lie back down without your assistance.

After the Cold. Often times, a bad cold or other illness can easily force your child's sleeping schedule out of whack. Whether it is the flu, a stomach virus, or something more severe, sleep separation should *always* take a back seat to any sort of illness. If your child is sick, he should be close to you. You always want to keep an eye on your little angel and be there to comfort him during his time of need. Many times, your child will wind up either sleeping in your bed or next to your bed during a sickness, and that's a good thing! Nobody should have a child far from them if he is sick. It is absolutely a time to nurture your child and to completely forget about any sleep issues.

Once the illness has fully run its course—it's quite a different story. When your child is healed of whatever it was that ailed him, get him back into his own room as soon as possible. Unfortunately, this is oft times easier said than done. Your little one will very quickly grow accustomed to being in mommy and daddy's arms all night, and won't be the slightest bit pleased about going back to his lonely little room.

Be mindful that it's easy to second guess your decision that your child is healed when he starts crying when you put him back into his crib. Just trust your intuition. If you think your baby is better, then he probably is. When he cries that first night back in his own room, it is probably only because he is frustrated that he cannot sleep with you anymore. Once again, you need to lay down the law and be strict. Once you're certain that your little one is no longer sick, you just need to let him cry it out a bit.

The length of time that your child has been sleeping in your room is likely to dictate how long it will take you to get him back to sleeping without you in his own room. If the illness lasted weeks, then it might take several nights of crying to get your little one back to peacefully sleeping on his own. If it's only been for a few nights, then it will probably either not be an issue at all or you might have only one or two short sessions of crying before you can have your nights back to yourself.

However long it takes you to get your child back into his room, be sure that you are unyielding and that you trust your intuition. If you have any doubts as to whether your little one is still sick, consult your pediatrician. But as soon as your child is better, get him out of your room and back into his.

Nighttime Fears. When your child is somewhere between two to three and a half years old, he might experience some level of night time fears. One night, when my oldest (and best sleeping) son was about three, he asked me if I could check to see if there was a monster under his bed. Within a week's time, he screamed in terror every time I even attempted to leave his room. He would come to our room completely terrified every night.

Nobody was getting any sleep, and my once wonderful sleeper was suddenly screaming and petrified all night long. I did some research into toddler terrors and tried some ideas, but nothing seemed to work. We tried a "monster flashlight", "monster spray", a "monster alarm", and even rationalizing, but all to no avail. No matter what book I read or what technique I tried, nothing worked. My son was in our room screaming every night.

Getting too far into this issue goes well beyond the scope of this book. I am not an expert in this field, but I would like to just say a couple things: The *only* thing that allowed any of us to get some sleep during these episodes was to let my poor little guy sleep in our room until his fears subsided. The more we tried to fight it and keep our son in his own room, the more aggravated his fears became. In fact, the only way that we were able to alleviate his fears was by allowing him to sleep in the safety and security of our presence. So, for a few months (yes, a few *months!*), we had a bed of blankets on the floor next to our bed, and together we rode out his storm of terrors.

Important to note here is that we didn't let him sleep in our bed. He was completely content on the floor next to us, and I was certain that allowing him in our bed would be a costly mistake. Also, having the blankets already set up on the floor waiting for him allowed us to avoid the need for me to wake up in the middle of the night to help him (can you tell how desperately I need my sleep?). We had a little bed set up on the floor and he could come in and sleep whenever he needed. He was instructed not to wake us unless he absolutely had to, and that he could just lie down on the floor and go to sleep.

The other thing I'd like to note is that night fears can be easily mistaken for manipulation to try to get in your bedroom at night. Children are very creative in coming up with reasons to get into your room after they are put to bed. They will come up with almost any excuse to try to weasel their way back into your room. Even to this day, our kids every now and then test the waters to see if they can somehow inch their way into our bedroom after they have been put to sleep.

When my son started with his fears, it didn't take me long to assess that he truly was petrified. The important thing for you to remember as a parent is that if your child is truly terrified, he is not trying to manipulate you. You need to help your toddler try to feel more secure during such a dark and scary time. I find it completely inappropriate to force a terrified child to stay in his room alone. Your job is to comfort your child and help to alleviate his fears; not to chastise him and force him to be alone! Although his fears might seem completely irrational to you, they are very real to him. So, be kind and sensitive if this problem does come your way, and just forget about the sleep issues for however long it takes to work through it.

If you happen to be one of the unlucky parents with a child experiencing nighttime terrors, there are many books out there that you can help you. There is also a vast amount of information regarding night terrors on the internet. But don't ever forget that you need to help your child through this period, and as always be a sensitive and loving parent.

CHAPTER REVIEW

(Make sure you understand the following concepts before moving onto the next chapter)

1. Recognize and overcome the various sleep issues that arise;
2. Learn how to deal with nighttime fears;
   – and –
3. Get your baby back to bed after an illness.

Chapter 7

Bed Ready

Y<small>OUR GOALS FOR THIS CHAPTER ARE</small>:

1. Determine whether your toddler is ready for a bed;
2. Prepare for the transfer;

– and –

3. Keep your toddler in his bed, and out of yours.

As your little one matures, you will eventually begin to wonder whether he is ready for a bed. If you're like most new parents, the thought of putting your child in a bed sounds like a thrilling endeavor. It's so exciting that you'll be ever so tempted to rush the change. *But don't!* If you put your little one in a bed too early, you'll wind up with whole slew of midnight roaming issues that you can avoid if you simply wait until he is actually ready. You will be giving your child a huge amount of freedom by putting him in a bed, and it could wind up costing you a great deal of your own freedom and many sleepless nights if you make the change too early.

Determining whether your toddler is ready for a bed depends on several factors. Age is one of them. Typically, the earliest that you'll want to make the change to a bed is when your child is around two-and-a-half years old. By that age, he theoretically will have the maturity to stay in his bed at your direction, and will be able to follow your rules pertaining to the new bed.

Sometimes you won't have the luxury of deciding when your child should go into a bed, as there may be other forces making the choice for you. You may have to make a premature transition in order to give the crib to a new sibling on the way.

Sometimes, as in our case, your child might make the decision for you. Our third son began crawling out of his crib when he was fifteen months old and there wasn't a thing we could do about it. He wasn't old enough to punish or even to reprimand. Our pediatrician recommended that we put a net over the top of the crib to keep him caged in like an animal, but my husband and I just couldn't (when I look back, I sometimes wish I had used the net).

After he fell out of the crib several times while trying to climb out, we basically were forced to put our fifteen month old into a bed so he wouldn't hurt himself. Not surprisingly, we wound up with many more sleep-deprived nights than we would have had we been able to wait longer. Our son was simply too young to listen to what we were saying, and we wound up paying for it dearly.

He paid no attention to our instructions, and was too young to even care about our warnings and reprimands. Nearly every night, that little angel of ours was wandering the house and we were exhausted. We finally put a gate up at his door and that made things a bit easier, but there were still a lot more sleepless nights than if he had still been in his crib. The moral of the story is that if you do have the luxury of choosing when to put your child in a bed, the important thing is to make sure that you wait until he is mature enough to listen and understand your rules for his new bed. If you can't wait, using a gate (or, yes—even a net) to keep your child contained is probably going to help your predicament.

There are certain questions that you can ask yourself in order to assess whether your child is ready to be transitioned into a bed: Can he follow directions well? Does he listen to you when you say "no"? Does he respond to your reprimands and understand consequences for his behavior? If you answer these questions in the affirmative, then your child is probably mature enough to be moved into a bed. If the toddler does not respond to your reprimands and warnings, and does not listen to directions well, then you might want to consider waiting another six months or so until he has the maturity to handle his new freedom. There's no great hurry, believe me.

Our first son moved into a bed when he was two years old, just before his new little brother was due to take over the crib. We transferred him to the bed about six weeks before my second one was due to arrive. We did it that way so that we wouldn't have to deal with any new bed issues on the night that our new baby came home.

It turned out to be a perfect time for our son to make the transition. He was able to listen to and abide by my rules, and understood my warnings about staying in bed. For the most part he was able to follow my instructions with very little objection, so the change went very smoothly.

Time for a change. When you do determine that your child is ready, there are some things you can do to try to ensure that he stays in his bed once he is put to sleep. As your child matures, preparation is the key for any kind of change that is going to occur—including moving into a new bed. If you let your toddler know what is expected of him *before* you institute a change, you can avoid a lot of potential problems. (This applies to all aspects of child rearing.)

So, lay the groundwork with your child when it's time for the new bed. Let him know way in advance that he will be getting his own bed soon and make it an exciting endeavor for him But at the same time let your child know that there are certain rules that he must follow if he wants to be a "big boy".

Make sure your toddler understands what the rules are before he even sees the new bed for the first time. Just like the sleeping issues when your child was younger, if you establish your desired behavior from the beginning, then you will not have to take the time later to undo the unwanted behavior that has developed. Lay down the law, and take the time and the energy to ensure that your child sticks by your guidelines.

Sometimes it's just a lot easier to turn the other cheek and ignore that your child has broken a rule or has behaved in some unwanted fashion. The second your child thinks that he can get away with a certain behavior, he will continue to behave in that manner unless and until you put an end to it. So, don't allow any unwanted behaviors to develop right from the start. Trust me, it's much easier this way. As always, being lazy in the short run will make things harder for you in the end.

During your preparation to move your child into a bed, make sure he understands that he's not allowed to get out of bed, and that he must call for you just like when he was in his crib. This will at least buy you a little bit of time before he begins to show up at your bedside at 5:30 in the morning, ready to start his day. When your toddler was in his crib and woke up early, he would probably (hopefully) just play there for a while before you had to go in and get him. When you transfer him into a bed, however, it is quite a different story. Now when your child wakes up, he has a new found power to simply get out of bed and walk into your room to wake you up. That is why it is important to try to keep your child in his bed (at least in the beginning), and try to keep him in his bed until you go to get him.

If your child wakes up painfully early, as many toddlers do, see if you can teach him to play quietly in his bed with some toys until he hears you awake or you call for him. Have some toys laid out for him next to his bed and instruct him to play with the toys in the morning. Give him a time period that he can understand—like, "don't come out until the sun comes up", or "don't get out of bed until I call for you, or come and get you". Define the parameters. Contrary to what you may think, it's not that difficult to teach a child to do this—so give it a try. If you don't like my new bed rules, that's fine. You can always make up your own guidelines to better suit your own family system.

Bed guards are a good idea to put on your toddler's new bed. Fit the guards on both sides when the child first starts to sleep there. This is not only for your child's safety, but it will also help to encourage him to stay in his bed. Remind your little one frequently that he must stay in his bed during the night, and continue to remind him of this for the first couple of months. Make sure that your child is not allowed to freely roam the house or come in to your room whenever he feels like it. Without the appropriate efforts to set guidelines in order to keep your toddler in his new bed (and out of yours), you will wind up like so many exhausted parents whose children slip into bed with them night after night.

The Midnight Roamer. I can assure you that no matter how much you prepare your toddler and warn him of the consequences, you will ultimately find him at your bedside one night at 3 a.m. Rather than dreading this midnight rendezvous, you should embrace his little visit as a pristine opportunity to teach your child that you mean business. Just scoop your young adventurer right up into your arms as soon as you see him at your bedside, and put him firmly back into his bed. Don't be nice. Don't smile. Don't even give him a kiss. Remind him that it is not okay for him to get out of bed, tuck him in quickly, and then leave.

If your child starts to cry, just reassure him that he's fine and leave the room. You want to make his little late night visit as unpleasant as possible. If your child cries for a couple of minutes, do not go back into his room. You'll regret if you go back in at this point, as your child will quickly learn that if he cries in his new bed he can get what he wants. If you just let him cry, he'll get over it quickly and will learn how to stay in his bed.

Be sure to remind your young one the next morning of the rules, and then repeat the same message to him when you put him to sleep. If you stick to your guns, it will be only a matter of a couple nights before he will figure out that you mean what you say. On the other hand, if you let your child crawl into bed with you and cuddle, then you can bet he'll be back the next night—and every night thereafter for that matter until you are able to put a halt to it. In the short run, the easiest thing for you to do is to just move over and make some room on your bed for him. It's tough to be up in the middle of the night, especially if you've gotten used to sleeping through the night for the last couple of years.

It's all too easy to fall prey to your toddler in the middle of the night, especially since they are just so cute when they show up at your bedside. You'll open your eyes to have that adorable little face staring at you, and as soon as you open your eyes a big smile will come across his face. At that moment you'll realize just how unbelievably cute your child is and you'll just want to scoop him up and cuddle with him. But *don't*. It's a trap! You will be sucked right into it if you're not careful. And on the fifty-seventh night in a row of your child tossing and turning in your bed next to you, you'll understand how truly stuck you are.

Early risers. No matter how diligent you are about making and enforcing strict bed rules, there will inevitably come a day when you can no longer make your child stay in his bed in the morning. It may come sooner or later, but I promise you it will come. Your toddler will eventually reach an age that it's just doesn't make sense to make him stay in his bed until you call for him or go to his room to get him.

When your child begins to wander around the house in the very early morning, see if you can at least keep him in his room until the sun comes up. This will buy you a little bit more sleeping time in the morning. Don't let yourself get into the habit of letting your child crawl into bed with you at five in the morning. Even though the cuddle will feel wonderful, if you let him come into your bed before it's light out, his bedside arrival time will be earlier and earlier as the days go by. Sooner than you know it, that little rascal will be crawling into your bed in the middle of night. So, if you love to cuddle with your kids (like I do), just lay down the law and do it only after sunrise.

If your child chronically wakes up at a painfully early hour, then try to get him in the routine of playing quietly until you wake up or until the sun begins come up. Some parents really don't mind letting their kids climb into bed with them at 5:30 a.m., and if you're one of them—more power to you! If you cannot keep your toddler out of your room before it's light out, as a last resort you can always teach him how to turn on the television and have it preset for a morning show until you wake up. (I must tell you that I am not a fan of television. In my opinion, most children watch way too much television, and it is a huge waste of a beautiful, young brain. So keep the TV at an absolute minimum, and use it only as a necessity.) Once your child is waking up after sunrise, nix the morning television watching altogether. It's nothing but another bad habit that develops all too easily. Whatever you do to keep your child out of your room when it's still dark outside, just don't allow any bad patterns to develop that you are ultimately going to want to undo.

Be Positive. One last thing that I'd like to add is that positive reinforcement is very important when you are trying to establish a desired behavior. This is especially true if you are trying to change a particular way that your child has been acting. For example, if you are having trouble getting your toddler to stay in bed, make sure that you reward him on the day that he does stay in bed all night. This reward can be a simple "thank you", or "good job", or any other form of praise for his accomplishment.

Make a big deal out of it when you get what you want from your child—it makes a huge difference in their behavior and attitude, and helps to build their self-confidence. You do not have to reward your child with a present in order to render effective positive reinforcement (although sometimes you might want to). Words of encouragement from a parent are huge for a child, and they will never tire of hearing praise from you. So make sure when your child does what you like, you let him know how very pleased you are.

Once again, this concept applies to all aspects of child-rearing, and not just to sleeping. *Be a cheerleader!* Make your kids feel great about themselves, and always let them know how wonderful they are. Tell them all the time how much you love them. Constant reinforcement for their good behavior is one of the best ways to accomplish this.

CHAPTER REVIEW

(Don't move onto the next chapter until you understand the following concepts)

1. Determine whether your toddler is mature enough to be moved into a bed;
2. Decide whether you are rushing the issue;
3. Understand how to prepare your toddler for the new bed;

– and –

4. Understand how to keep your baby in his new bed.

Chapter 8

Putting your Baby
on a Schedule

YOUR GOALS FOR THIS CHAPTER ARE:

1. Understanding the benefits of scheduled feedings;

– and –

2. Determining whether it's right for you and your child.

As a new parent, you are certain to encounter a multitude of people with a veritable plethora of opinions on how you should handle your new baby. Some will insist that you get your child on a feeding schedule, while plenty of others will tell you the exact opposite.

Personally, I think that the decision to put your baby on schedule depends on you and your individual situation. If you feel the need for a schedule or if you feel that your baby needs it, do it. Your little one can and will adapt to whatever you implement. If you decide not to put him on a schedule, I can promise you that it will not be a fatal omission.

I put my first son on a feeding schedule on his first day home from the hospital. I fed him every three hours—6 a.m., 9 a.m., noon, and so on, and then my last feeding (well, hopefully my last) was somewhere around 9 p.m. I woke him up if he was sleeping to feed him, except during the night, and the schedule worked very well for the two of us. With my second child, I pretty much did the same thing, but was not quite as rigid.

By the time my last bundle of joy came into the picture, it was just too overwhelming for me to try to keep it together enough to stay on any sort of schedule. Merely keeping my head above water at that point was about all I could do. The mere thought of trying to keep my third baby on a schedule while tending to my other two young boys was just a bit too much for me to bear.

If you have the desire and/or the inclination, and no other toddlers to contend with, then a schedule really can be helpful. I do not, however, find it to be crucial to the success of getting your child to sleep through the night. My third son, who had nothing that even remotely resembled a schedule, slept through the night at seven weeks.

Many children, and many parents for that matter, function better with the added structure of a clearly defined routine. You will get to know your own child, and you will quickly figure out if he (or you) is one of these people. In the midst of all of the chaos of a newborn in the house, some people (and some babies for that matter) crave some level of control in their lives. A schedule can help to provide that control, to some extent at least. So, feel it out and see if you're one of them. Figure out what works best for you and your baby and go with it.

There is one situation where I do believe that a schedule can be very beneficial. If you've waited a number months to begin the Sleep Baby Sleep method, a schedule is a great way to help your child to sleep without your help. A schedule can be particularly helpful if you've been nursing your baby around the clock. Chapter 5 has more detail on implementing a schedule for an older baby.

CHAPTER REVIEW

(Don't move onto the next chapter until you understand the following concepts)

1. Is scheduling right for your baby and you?
2. Is your baby the scheduling type? And
3. Can scheduling fit into your family's needs?

Conclusion

I hope that I have provided you with some very helpful, yet relatively simple techniques for teaching your child how to sleep though the night. The Sleep Baby Sleep process is uncomplicated and concise, and if you stick with it your baby *will* sleep better and longer. The techniques in this book will make your child *and you*, happier and better rested. Additionally, the logic set forth in these pages, when applied to any aspect of your parent/child relationship, will help you to develop a well-behaved, disciplined, respectful and self-reliant child.

The driving theme in this book is that you can empower your little one with the independence to be able to sleep without you. As you gradually separate yourself from your child during sleep times, he will learn how to pacify himself and to be in charge of his own sleeping. Once your child can sleep by himself, then you can find some time for yourself. Having your own breathing space enables you to be a better parent and allows you to have the time for yourself and the time for the other important relationships in your life. Take the time to ensure that you get your own privacy. If you do this, then you will be a more complete person and therefore a much better parent.

On the other hand, if you allow your baby to take up every ounce of your available energy, then the other parts of your life will inevitably suffer. Sacrifice too much for your children, and you will eventually become angry, resentful, and not to mention chronically exhausted. You will feel cheated and ultimately your relationship with your children will suffer, which is something you do not want to let happen.

Remember that there's nothing to feel guilty about. You can be a great parent even though you make your child sleep in another room! Making the supreme sacrifice of giving up every minute of your life for your children does *not* make you a good parent, especially if you grow cranky and resentful. Even if you have to make your child cry it out once in a while to establish the behavior that you want, it doesn't make you a bad parent. I promise you that you will be a better parent and your children will be better adjusted if you have your own space and time.

So, good luck to you on what is certain to be one of the most amazing journeys of your lifetime. Give your children lots of love and caring at every opportunity, but remember—sleep without them!

The End

Printed in the United States
30546LVS00002B/102